A MAN AND HIS CAR

by

Felix J. Vialet, Jr.

Dr. Jackie S. Henderson
Your Family Research & Publishing
Stone Mountain, Georgia

ISBN-13: 978-1532741760

ISBN-10: 1532741766

Dedication

I wrote this book as a tribute to my father who passed in October 2000 as a family man and a business man. I presented the story as it was told to me and as I remember the facts. Writing this book also enabled me to reflect on the wonderful experiences of my childhood and realize their impact on my adult life. Unfortunately, three individuals in the book are no longer here to read and enjoy it. My mother Huldah passed in 2013, my aunt Elise passed in 2014, and my brother Aubrey passed in 2015. I sincerely hope that this story serves as an inspiration to all.

With deep respect and love, I honor my parents, Felix "Skip" Sr. and Huldah Vialet; grandparents, Louis Flavel and Elsa Vialet; and my great-grandparents, Antoine and Marie Eleanor Vialet. They truly believed in the pursuit of business entrepreneurship and leadership. Special recognition and thanks to my wonderful family and generous friends for the information received while researching the life of my father for this book.

The warmest gratitude extended to my Aunt Elise Vialet, and cousins Janice Fraites and Ulrica "Ricci" Vialet. Aunt Elise is much a part of my father's dreams and prosperous journey. She was always by his side, bravely encouraging and voluntarily assisting his every business venture. "Ricci's" assistance with research and emails of wit and wisdom was beneficial to this text.

I wish to thank my wife, Marie Eleanor Vialet, for giving compassionate patience, encouragement, faith, unwavering support, and her preliminary editing and typing of my initial transcript.

I especially wish to thank Estelle Ford Williamson, Writing Instructor, at the Lou Walker Senior Center in Georgia for her guidance and support on this literary project.

Lastly, I am eternally indebted to my cousin, Dr. Murdisia Orr, for her advice, critical text reading, editorship, invaluable time, and steadfast support throughout this arduous journey to bring fruition to this book.

CONTENTS

Photos

Introduction

Virgin Islands
Coat of Arms

The story in this book takes place on the island of St. Thomas, one of the three United States Virgin Islands. The other United States Virgin Islands (U.S.V.I.) are St. Croix and St. John.

St. Thomas is a thirty-two square mile island whose beauty can "take your breath away." The temperature ranges from approximately 72 degrees to 87 degrees with a mild trade wind blowing constantly. Beautiful blooming flora and fauna cascade from the mountainsides. One can say that the land is one gigantic botanical garden surrounded by sandy beaches and crystal-clear water.

The United States bought the Virgin Islands from Denmark for twenty-five million dollars in 1917, to help protect The Panama Canal. United States citizenship was granted to inhabitants of the islands in 1927. The Navy governed the islands until 1931. The Organic Act of 1936, allowed for the creation of a senate, and the political process evolved. The Department of Interior appointed a governor until 1970, when the islanders elected their first governor.

Due to World War II, the need to protect the Caribbean seas and access to the Panama Canal increased. The Navy built a Sub Marine Base with docking facilities in one cove of the island for submarines and large cruisers. They also constructed living quarters for soldiers. Construction and public works' projects created many jobs for the islanders. Post-war era saw an increase in the number of tourists to the island. People were looking for new vacation spots, especially places with sandy beaches, coral reefs, and blue turquoise water. The Virgin Islands had these treasures in abundance and tourists had begun to frequent the island.

The development of the tourist business began on St. Thomas and later expanded to St. Croix and St. John. St. Thomas was the seat of government for all three islands and the town of Charlotte Amalie was the center for Navy operations. The Navy sailors called St. Thomas "Rock City" because it is essentially one big mountain.

Visible on the island are homes with bright red corrugated tin roofs set into the steep hillside. Lush green plants, trees, and tropical flowers add to the beauty of the island. Cruise ships began to add St. Thomas as a regular port of call and the airline industry began to grow. Large planes flew into Puerto Rico and passengers going to the other islands, including St. Thomas were shuttled by smaller planes to their destinations. This new tourist trade brought prosperity and growth in areas of home and hotel construction, real estate, jewelry and liquor sales.

Today, the Virgin Islands offer one of the highest standards of living in the Caribbean. The increase of the tourist industry in St. Thomas also created the need for a better transportation system, thus, this is where my father played a major role.

Family History

My paternal great-grandparents, Antoine and Marie Eleanor Vialet, had four children: Christopher, Beatrice, Flavel, and Wilfred. My grandfather, Louis Flavel Vialet, was born on January 5, 1883. My grandfather, his sister, and his brothers lost their parents at a young age.

His uncle-in-law, Justin Burnet, raised my grandfather. My grandfather affectionately called Flavel by family and friends, was well trained in cabinetry, and loved by many people. He was an ambitious, kind, and intelligent young man. Although he had a limited formal education, not too many could match his mental mathematical ability.

Flavel was a cabinet-maker and a carpenter. He learned the craft of cabinet making from his uncle, Justin Burnet. He became one of the most outstanding cabinet-makers on the islands.

Handmade Dresser by Flavel Vialet

"Grandpa" as I called him, was so imaginative, that he could take an intricate furniture design, cut it out on cardboard, and use it to shape the hard mahogany with his hand tools. Hand-made cabinet designing and construction was one of his specialties. A few of these valuable hand-made pieces were shipped across the Atlantic to Europe. Some of my grandfather's works are in a museum in Copenhagen, Denmark.

Pieces of his furniture could be found in homes of some prominent families such as Chinnery, Bornn, Paiewonsky, and Petersen. Many mahogany pieces were also placed on pulpits and hand railings of many churches. His work also included making jalousie windows and storm shutters. Finally, yet importantly, he took delight and pride in building coffins. My grandfather built his own coffin to ensure that it was constructed of the best workmanship. However, the family disliked the idea of a coffin waiting for his use; and therefore, its disposal was encouraged.

Grandpa was a very good dancer. He taught such dances as Quadrille, Polka, Mazurka, and other round dances. Through his love of music and dancing, he met his wife, Elsa George. He loved to have a good time with music and dance. When he took Elsa as his wife, he took his vows very seriously. He called her "Lush" and never allowed her to go to the grocery store to shop alone. He had someone deliver the goods to the house or he shopped for the items his wife needed. His desire was to have his wife remain at home and to take care of the family.

My grandmother, Elsa George Vialet, the daughter of my maternal grandparents Esther Seisman and Augustus George, was born in St. Thomas in 1886. During her teen years, she lived in Haiti. She had two sisters, Asta and Rita, and a brother, Julious Hill. "Grannie" as I called her, gave birth to thirteen children: Jose Hidalgo, Lionel, Louis, Rudolph, Elise, Felix, Flavel, Susthen, Audrey, Theodore, and Aubrey.

Louis Flavel and Elsa George Vialet
(Felix's Parents)

Two children had died soon after birth. She worked very hard to raise her family. I can remember my grandmother leaving the house only on Sunday mornings at 5: 45 a.m. to walk to the Anglican Church, which was less than four city blocks from her house.

Grannie was a Christian who instilled in her children that God came first in their lives. When my grandfather became disillusioned in his later years because he was not paid regularly for his hard cabinetry work, she never gave up on him and her children. She remained with her family, providing guidance and love, which was desperately needed at this point in their lives. She supported her husband at home and in the family business.

Even though Grannie was not Catholic, she insisted her children have instruction in the Catholic faith and obtain an education. Devoutly religious, she attended church every Sunday.

Raising her children and caring for the home was her main concern. To support her family, she smoothed cabinets with sandpaper and weaved straw chairs that were later sold.

A weaved straw chair by Elsa

My grandmother was the true matriarch of her family. Grannie never sought recognition or fame. She exuded happiness, practiced charity, and taught her children and grandchildren to use their skills for self-fulfillment and achievement. All of us were happy and pleased to bring home friends because she had a way of making them feel at home by sharing whatever we had with them.

Later in life, one daughter and six sons left the island of St. Thomas. One daughter and three sons remained on the island. My aunts and uncles thanked God for giving their nieces and nephews great parents who loved them and provided guidance. They also helped the children to understand there was a Supreme Being who should be worshiped, cherished, and obeyed.

My grandfather was an aspiring young man. Despite his limited education, he had foresight to buy property that my Aunt Elise owns today. There were four houses on the Vialet property. In 1916, a hurricane destroyed one of the homes and damaged the other three. Grandpa rebuilt and repaired the damaged houses. Unfortunately, a hurricane in 1924 destroyed another house. Again, he rebuilt the house. In 1940, a third house was lost in a fire. This time he and his sons rebuilt that house with concrete blocks instead of wood.

My grandfather toiled mightily. His type of carpentry work was not easy to construct by hand. After he had completed a set of furniture, he would be told by customers that payment would be made in installments. Soon a few of his customers were late in payments for completed jobs. These financial occurrences made him bitter, angry, and sad, especially when they interfered with his family's economic welfare.

My aunts and uncles felt that their father became disillusioned with life when mounting financial concerns and natural disasters destroyed his family property. Frustrated by his inability to provide the wealth and comfort for his family, he began to use alcohol that caused further strains on his relationship with his wife and children. These setbacks may have also prevented him from expanding his business.

Despite my grandfather's shortcomings, he loved his family and provided for them the best that he could. My grandfather departed this life on December 13, 1946, and my grandmother passed on November 12, 1954. May God grant them eternal peace.

My Father's Early Years

Felix, Sr. was obsessed with the automobile. As a young boy growing up, his room was filled with books and pictures of cars. He would tell his brothers and friends that one day he was going to buy himself a car. They told him to give up that dream, but he would just smile and say, "wait." He was a slender and well-dressed young man with big aspirations and dreams. Felix admired his father Flavel. He knew his father was a master of cabinetry and woodworking, a self-made man in charge of his own destiny, and his own boss.

My father's dream was also to be his own boss and he began working with his father to learn the trade of making hand-made cabinets, jalousie windows, and furniture. My father learned the cabinetry trade so well that he began to get his own customers. Felix was only paid when his father was paid for big jobs they worked on together. Felix knew if he was going to make it on his own and be able to afford the things he dreamed about, he would have to get a part time job to accomplish these things.

All the Vialet boys learned different aspects of hand-made woodworking of furniture from their father. Most of the brothers enjoyed drinking, dancing, smoking, womanizing, and gambling. However, Felix refrained from drinking alcohol and smoking cigarettes because he said that it made one "lose his cool" and he needed to keep his composure at all times. Despite the differences in entertainment, Felix looked up to his brothers, and they in turn looked out for him.

My Uncle Lionel was the first entrepreneur in the family. He had two houses, a restaurant, and barbershop. He was a barber and a police officer by profession. When speaking of my Uncle Lionel, my father always referred to him as "the barber." Louis was my favorite uncle. He was a tailor. My uncles, Lionel and Louis, educated my father in craps, games of chance, and poker. After some extensive training, they allowed him to join one or two of their poker games. Felix did well from the start. He had a knack for reading facial expressions, and in addition, was very lucky.

Felix learned how to play the game of pool in his brother's restaurant. My Uncle Lionel had a pool table in one corner of his restaurant. My father would stop on his way home every night to practice. Pool playing turned out to be his money tree. He began to frequent the places where there were games of chance. It soon became very profitable for him. His money roll started to grow rapidly.

In approximately three months, my father had won over eight thousand dollars. He was able to repay his brothers with interest who fronted him for gambling fees. Felix did not put his money in local banks, but rather placed it into two of his mother's Bibles. In between every other page of the Bibles, starting from page seven, he would place a one-hundred-dollar bill. He began this habit with his first win of three thousand dollars. From then on, every time he made a big score, he would add to the Bibles.

For safekeeping, the Bibles were placed in different places. One Bible was placed in the bottom of a china cabinet in the main house; the other Bible was put high up in the rafters of his bedroom, which was separated from the main house. As the winnings grew, he added more Bibles. Although he knew gambling was not the best way to make a living, because there were some losing days as well, it helped him to save money.

Soon Felix found a part-time job with a wholesaler known as the "Dane Man" who sold dry goods, tea, coffee, sugar, rice, flour, salt, black pepper, corn meal, whole corn, chickpeas, and salt fish packed in rock salt. Although most of these items were sold directly to small grocery stores, there were also quite a few walk-in customers. The "Dane Man" hired him, but he could only give him three days a week part time to start. The pay was not too good but to make up the difference, he was given dry goods from the store.

Felix continued to work with his father in the mornings, and went to work with the "Dane Man" in the afternoons. He learned the wholesale business so fast that in about two to three months, he was working full time. His boss liked him and since my father knew most of the shopkeepers, he allowed Felix to give credit to those he trusted to pay their grocery bill every two weeks. He did very well and saved a large portion of his earnings. He worked for the "Dane Man" from 1939 through 1940.

Late one afternoon at work, Felix heard the fire truck siren headed toward Garden Street. He turned to one of the people in the store and said, "It's headed my way. I hope it is not my house." A short while later his niece came into the store to get him. She said, "Uncle, the big house burned to the ground." His reply was, "Oh my God!" He then ran up to Garden Street.

When he arrived at the house, there was nothing left. He made a quick check to be sure that everyone was out and no one was hurt. He looked at the charred rubble that was once the living room and located the area of the china cabinet that contained the Bible with his concealed money. The Bible and money were burnt to ash.

Although Felix was upset he had lost his earnings, he was more concerned for the safety of his family. As he entered the kitchen area where his family members had gathered, he asked his father if he had any idea of what they were going to do about sleeping arrangements. At that same moment, a neighbor, Mrs. Watlington, offered rooms in her home for the four girls until things were later settled.

Felix told his father that he had money saved and that he would use it for material to rebuild the house. He was sure that his brothers would also contribute to help rebuild the home. The boys and their father worked hard in rebuilding the big house. They built it with concrete blocks and wood. They were proud of their good work and their mother loved the new house.

Felix spent quite a bit of his time working. Young women considered him a good prospect for a husband. They had known he always held a job, dressed well, and kept a few dollars in his pocket. However, Felix was attentively fascinated with one young woman named Huldah Innis. She lived with her aunt in the section of town known as Savan. Huldah's mother and father were divorced. Although her mother had moved to Puerto Rico, her father remained in St. Thomas. After several dates, Felix wanted to move out of his parent's home and get his own apartment with Huldah.

A friend who worked at the Naval Sub Base informed Felix that there was an available job opening at the base. The Navy had just built a new game room in the building across from the airport on Bourne Field and would need someone to maintain it. He advised him to apply promptly if he was interested. Felix caught a ride to the sub base that afternoon and filled out an application. The clerk at the desk informed him that he could return in a week to check on the status of his application. All that week he was anxious. He could hardly wait until Friday to return to the base and check his status. Friday, when he returned, the clerk informed Felix that the captain wanted to meet with him.

The Navy Captain described the responsibilities of the job, which included maintaining the bar, card tables, ping-pong tables, pool tables and four bowling lanes. The Navy Captain asked my father if he thought that he could handle the job. My father assured the captain that although he had never seen a bowling ball or alley, he was a fast learner, and if given the job opportunity, he would make the captain proud. My father was given the job and was instructed to report to Bourne Field at 8:00 a.m. the following Monday morning.

Felix thanked the captain and went back to Savan to tell his girlfriend Huldah his good news. This full time job with the Navy would pay him much more money than he was making with the "Dane Man." This additional money would help pay for items needed for the apartment without using too much of his own savings. At this time, he did not divulge to his girlfriend anything about the money he had won at games of chance.

However, he knew he would eventually have to reveal to his girlfriend how he had received these extra earnings. He then headed to his parents' home on Garden Street to share his good job news and impending plans to move into his own apartment with Huldah. When he arrived, he was greeted by Teddy, his German shepherd dog, the family watchdog. It was so late that he did not have an opportunity to tell his parents his good news or future plans that evening.

The next day he awoke early. He informed his family of his plans for his future. He revealed his feelings about his girlfriend,

Huldah Innis. His mother said, "So that is why you are always in Savan." She wanted to know if they planned to get married. Felix informed her that they were going to wait to get married. However, they would be sharing an apartment.

His Mother wanted further information about this young woman and her family. His mother requested that he bring his girlfriend to meet the family. He told his mother Huldah lived in Savan with her aunt. Her father was a shoemaker who owned a shop on Back Street, and her mother lived in Puerto Rico. He promised his mother to bring his girlfriend by the house soon.

He then told his father that he was starting a full-time job with the Navy at 8:00 a.m. on Monday. This meant that he would only be able to work with his father on weekends. His father was happy for him and wanted to know the responsibilities of the new job. Felix had his usual breakfast of a bowl of hot cereal, a big slice of dumb-bread, a piece of salt fish, and a cup of tea. He fed his dog, then left to start the search for an apartment and inform the "Dane Man" that he had accepted a full time job with the Navy. Felix expressed to his former boss how much he enjoyed working with him and his appreciation for everything he had done for him.

It was early on a Saturday morning and the main street was still quiet. The merchants were just opening up their stores and putting out their goods. Felix proceeded to Savan to meet Huldah. He walked pass the Market Square which was busy with folks shopping for fresh fruits and vegetables. He arrived at Huldah's house and asked her to go with him to look for an apartment. They walked out to the road and towards apartments near an area close to where her cousin also lived. Felix and Huldah found a one-bedroom apartment that they both liked. He paid the manager rent of fifty dollars for the first month, received a receipt, and permission to move in anytime they were ready.

Although Huldah had pots and pans, silverware, dishes, linen, and other household items for the apartment, she was concerned about furniture. Felix assured her that he would go right away to purchase a bed frame and mattress. Felix's father agreed to help him make two dressers, a kitchen table, and four chairs. There was so much to do. My father installed new locks on the apartment doors and gave Huldah keys so that she could start cleaning before the furniture was delivered. He also gave Huldah money to have her cousin help her get the apartment ready. Felix told Huldah that on the following Friday after work, he would take her to meet his family.

Working on the Navy Base

Felix reported to his new job at 7:45 a.m. on Monday morning. His new boss, Corporal Butler, greeted him. The men exchanged pleasantries and then proceeded to review the duties and responsibilities of the job. They examined the equipment and discussed the maintenance of the game room. The two men developed a great friendship.

For approximately two months, Navy Corporal Butler trained Felix to manage the game room. Eventually, my father was able to manage the game room. After a month on the job, Felix began to teach the corporal how to play pool. The corporal was a fast learner and was interested in becoming a better pool player.

Pool Tournament in Game Room of Navy Base

Working on the Navy base, Felix learned how to bowl while in the game room. In the afternoon before waxing the bowling lanes, he would set up the pins on all four lanes and bowl about ten games. Felix always completed his work first and then vigorously practiced bowling or shooting pool. He would practice the same shot for days at a time until he could almost do it with his eyes closed.

Then he would move on to another shot. He would rack the balls and try to run the table for five games every other day. He became so good at pool that the soldiers could not beat him. Soldiers were brought to the game room from other ships to play against him. Soon my father competed in pool tournaments that earned him additional money.

Felix learned how to drive a car on the Navy base, and was determined to purchase a car for himself. Approximately six months after Felix began working in the game room, Corporal Butler received Navy orders to return state side. He came to the game room to say goodbye. He told Felix how much he enjoyed working with him. Felix thanked him for his guidance and friendship. Felix continued working for the Navy until the purchase of his first automobile changed his way of life.

Meeting the Family

That Friday after work, he went by Huldah's house. She was sitting there dressed and waiting for him. This was finally the day that she was going to meet his family. They walked to Back Street chatting as they walked. Huldah filled him in on the progress of the apartment. She and her cousin had cleaned up the apartment and hung curtains. The bed had been delivered and put together. He talked about his new job.

When they arrived at his family's home on Garden Street, Felix opened the gate to let Huldah into the yard. He had forgotten about Teddy, his dog, who automatically attacked any stranger entering the yard. Before Felix could stop him, Teddy jumped on Huldah, inflicting a small cut under her eye. Teddy retreated when he saw Felix. Huldah was trembling with fear.

The commotion aroused everyone who was in the house. Felix's mother rushed out to see what had occurred, and immediately took Huldah inside to cleanse the wound. She assured Huldah that it was not a severe cut.

Felix's mother said to Huldah with concern, "I am very sorry this happened on your first visit to my home, and I really hope it does not stop you from coming by any time." She also inquired as to how Huldah was doing in setting up the new apartment. Huldah confirmed that things were progressing nicely. As Huldah was preparing to leave, Felix's dad approached her and told her how pleased he was to meet her. He told her that he hoped that she and Felix would be happy together.

Moving Into the First Apartment

The apartment was almost ready. It was clean and had frilly curtains hung on the windows. The bed and mattress were delivered and in its place. Felix was anxious to complete the hand-making of furniture for his new apartment. He was pleasantly surprised when he arrived at his father's workshop one afternoon to find that his dad had finished the dresser and two chairs. Felix thanked his father for his help and proceeded to work on completing the kitchen table and other two chairs.

Next, he had his brother Hidalgo add mahogany stain onto all the furniture. Within a week, the furniture was ready. Felix secured a truck and men to help deliver the furniture. He informed Huldah as to what time the furniture was to arrive so that she would be at the apartment for the delivery. After arranging for the furniture delivery, he went to the power company to have the electricity turned on. He then returned to the apartment to see if the furniture had been delivered. Everything was in place.

As Felix looked around the bedroom, he told Huldah that he would make a head and footboard for the bed later on. He also expressed that before they moved in, he wanted to have a priest come to bless the apartment She told him that she had already arranged for a priest to come to bless their new home. By that following Monday, the priest came and blessed the apartment. In August of 1940, Felix and Huldah moved into their first apartment.

Huldah and Felix

The First Vehicle

In 1941, Felix fulfilled one of his dreams and bought his first car, a Studebaker Commander. The exterior was light green with double silver chrome molding around the entire length of the car. The interior was a dark tan. There was a radio with many shiny buttons. The entire interior lit up whenever the doors opened. It was a beautiful car. The silver streak molding along the sides of the car eventually became the name and logo of Felix's first business venture.

Felix and 1st Silver Streak Vehicle

He had finally saved enough money from his job and the extra earnings from his pool games to make a cash purchase for his first car. He was the first to own a vehicle in his family. His sister Elise was the first to see him drive up to his parents' home. She called out to the rest of the family to come out to see the new car.

His mother peeked out from the window and his dad came out from his workshop. Everyone was excited and congratulated Felix on this grand accomplishment. His sister insisted that she be the first one to get a ride in the new car. His family did not envy his desire for a car because he always monetarily provided for his family.

Felix left his parent's home and drove down Main Street very slowly towards his home in Savan. He wanted everyone to see his new car. He caused quite a commotion when he drove up to his apartment and tooted his horn. He walked inside to get Huldah, but she was not at home. He assumed that she was visiting her aunt.

He caused more excitement when he arrived at the aunt's house. Huldah was so pleased and excited. She was ready in a flash to go for her first ride. When they returned to their apartment Felix said to Huldah, "I have accomplished one of two goals. One goal was to own a car and the other is to be my own boss."

The next day his brothers came to see the car and congratulate him. By this time, everyone on Garden Street had heard about Felix's car. Many people wanted a ride in the car since they had never ridden in a car before. He decided to charge a quarter for a ride from Garden Street to the Market Square and back to defray the expense of gas. He made ten dollars on the first day. Little did he realize that this was the formation of his Silver Streak Taxi Service.

Shuttle Taxi Service Commences

That night, Felix sat in his apartment thinking about how easy it had been to make ten dollars for gas. If he could make fifteen or twenty dollars a day with his car, he could make a good living and would not have to work for anyone but himself. That idea really resonated in his mind.

The next morning before going to work, he drove by his parent's house to check in on everyone. As he was about to leave, his sister Elise asked him to drop her off to work. Eventually this became a daily routine. His sister and many other women in the neighborhood were very active in the community and were members of many organizations.

Soon, his sister's friends inquired about securing rides in Felix's car to work and other locations. Felix saw this as an opportunity to attain his dream of self-employment. He knew that in order to take the women to work in the mornings, he would need to adjust his working hours. He discussed his idea of a revised work schedule with the captain at the Navy Sub Base. Felix was successful in getting a favorable schedule that accommodated his new driving routine.

He informed Huldah that he would get home much later now that his work schedule had changed. Felix also had to contact his prospective clients to arrange fees and pick-up times. Within a few weeks, word of his car service spread within the community and there were increased requests from other individuals. Due to his busy schedule, it soon became difficult for prospective customers to reach Felix to arrange for additional services.

Felix then decided that he needed a telephone and a central location for the operation of his car service business. He asked his father for permission to build a small office on his home property. His father not only gave permission, but also promised to help with the construction of a space in front of the family kitchen. Felix envisioned his second goal, to begin a business and be his own boss, become a reality. Felix started his business with an office, a car, and a telephone. The office was referred to as the "Station."

Soon requests for car services were too much for a part time venture. It had become time to give up his full time job on the Navy base. Felix spoke to the Captain and informed him of his plans and the need to submit his resignation with two weeks' notice. He thanked the Captain for several opportunities that the job had provided. The Captain wished him well in his endeavors.

Felix had his eye on a discarded pool table that was in good condition in the Navy recreation center. He asked the Captain if it was possible to purchase the pool table. The Captain agreed to the purchase arrangement. With this acquisition, Felix was ensured that he would be able to keep his pool shooting skills intact.

Felix soon realized that his taxi service needed additional cars and drivers in order to meet the increased demands of his growing business and clientele. He visited the local dealerships to survey available cars and to determine who would offer the best sale deals. He had enough cash to make a substantial down payment but needed to negotiate financing of a loan for the remainder of the cost.

Although he could have afforded to pay all cash, Felix thought it best to keep some cash on hand in case of an emergency. During his interview of prospective drivers, he looked for individuals who were trustworthy, possessed good driving skills, and were quick learners.

With the addition of three cars and three drivers, Silver Streak Taxi Service became an actuality. The telephone number, "333" was catchy and easy to remember. The pool table was placed in the middle of the Station. It served several purposes besides pool games. When the pool table was covered with plywood, it became available desk space or used for ping-pong games.

Phone calls for taxi service were managed by an available driver or a family member whenever the drivers were out on a service call. Requests for the following day car service were placed on a blackboard hung on one wall. Calls for service were written on an index card and placed on the driver's clipboard. This system assisted Felix with a daily account of the number of jobs each driver completed and then compared the card with the amount of cash submitted. Each driver received fifty percent of what he earned for the week.

The business usually operated from 7 a.m. to 6 p.m. Monday through Saturday. Felix handled any calls on Sunday. Soon he had requests from three businesses, two hotels and the telephone company, to transport employees to and from work. This meant that a driver had to be assigned to the evening shift each week.

As the business progressed, Felix employed his sister Elise to manage the accounting books for the growing business. She collected the cash daily, completed the payroll, made bank deposits, and paid bills incurred by the business. Felix continued to add cars and drivers as the business needs increased.

Learning History of the Island and Sightseeing Tours

The purchase of seven cars enhanced Felix's business. The acquisition of additional cars allowed Felix to meet the growing customer demands and thoughts of expanding business to provide additional services. The growing tourist industry in St. Thomas offered new challenges and opportunities. Felix wanted to add sightseeing tours for visitors to explore the island to his growing business ventures.

Felix began preparations for this new sightseeing venture. He needed to become more knowledgeable of the island history, identification of appropriate places for tours, and best routes to show case the beauty of the island and its magnificent views. His sister brought him books on the history of the Virgin Islands from the library.

Felix read a book every evening. He wrote cue cards with pertinent historical information. He had Huldah quiz him to test his retention of the material studied. Initially he also used his cue cards to train and quiz a few drivers conducting visitor tours. Eventually this would become part of the training for all drivers. He made maps of two possible routes for tours and asked the drivers to help make the best selection.

Individual customers, hotel workers, and private businesses who needed shuttle service kept weekly revenue coming in, but the sightseeing business started to grow rapidly. Felix soon visualized the possibility of working with travel agencies to have tourists reserve sightseeing tours prior to their arrival to the island.

Growth of Silver Streak
Taxi Service

As people on the island of St Thomas started to rely more on car services offered by Silver Streak, the hours of operation extended an additional two hours from 9 p.m. until 11 p.m. At first, whoever was available at the Station would answer the phone but as the business grew, it became necessary to hire someone to take calls and record reservations.

The taxi service was providing an organized choice of transportation for the community. Felix took great pride in the type of car service provided by his business. Other individuals started to provide taxi service, but no one was as well organized or operative as Silver Streak. Eventually, small groups of taxi drivers started to congregate in various parts of the city such as outside grocery stores, Post Office, or the Market Place to get customers.

One evening, Huldah suggested that Felix do something to distinguish Silver Streak Taxis from all of the other individual taxis. She suggested that he should have a sign or symbol painted on his cars to make them more easily identifiable. Felix went to bed thinking about this proposition.

The next morning when he arrived at the station, he sat down with a writing pad and sketched out a sign that he thought would be appropriate for his cars. He decided that he wanted a sign placed atop the roof of each car with the name Silver Streak Taxi. He also designed a silver streak as an image to be placed as a logo through the Silver Streak Taxi name on the driver and passenger doors of each vehicle.

Felix obtained the name and address of a company in Puerto Rico that made roof top signs for cars. He sent the company a telegram describing what he envisioned and requested pertinent information needed to have the signs constructed. The reply from the company in Puerto Rico requested he send a sketch of the taxi sign and a deposit of fifty dollars. Felix wanted the sign in a rounded shape of a half-moon with the name "Silver Streak" in an arch across the top and the word "Taxi" below in the center. He wanted the sign to light up at night.

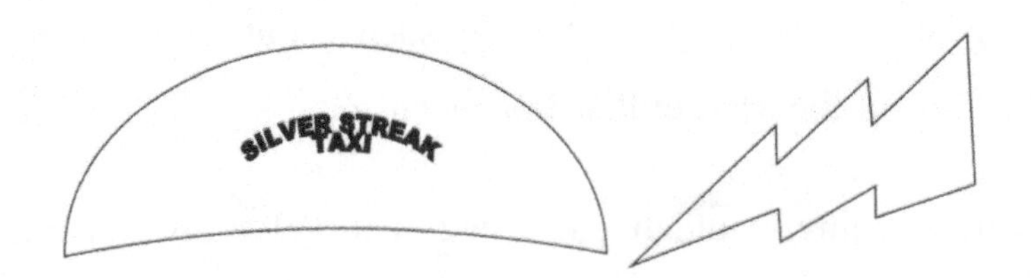

Roof top sign for Silver Streak taxies

Next, he contacted one of the best sign painters on the island, Mr. Hatchet. Felix and Mr. Hatchet had ongoing friendly rival wagers on baseball games. Mr. Hatchet was the only St. Louis Cardinals fan on the island and Felix was a huge New York Yankees fan. So far, that season the Yankees had won more games than the Cardinals, but Mr. Hatchet was determined, that his team would eventually win and he would recoup his losses.

Felix asked Mr. Hatchet what he would charge to paint the Silver Streak Taxi logo on the driver and passenger side doors of his vehicles. Mr. Hatchet looked at the sketch and asked Felix to select the font that he liked the most. Mr. Hatchet compiled figures at his desk and said it would cost twenty-five dollars per door for the painted signs he requested.

Felix paused for a few minutes, gave a sly smile, and agreed the cost sounded fair. He then said to Mr. Hatchet, "I am up four hundred dollars in the pool. That should cover the cost to paint all seven of my cars with fifty dollars left in pool wage." Mr. Hatchet smiled and said, "Yes, you are correct. You got me good this time."

Mr. Hatchet came to the station the next morning and began painting the logo onto the first car. When he completed his paintings, the car doors looked distinguished. Everyone who passed by the cars on Garden Street stopped and admired the signs on the doors. The roof top signs arrived within a few weeks from Puerto Rico. They were installed in time for the Christmas holidays. Silver Streak Taxis with its distinct logos and decorated with colored lights for the holidays were the talk of the town. Huldah had every reason to be proud of her brilliant idea.

It was now about three months since the bombing of Pearl Harbor and the United States and England were engaged in the war. Felix started to prepare for the shortage of certain items. The Islands depended on the majority of its dry goods to be brought in by ships and the war itself caused a hardship and shortage all around, the Islands not being an exception. Felix was most concerned about the shortage of oil and gasoline. He could start to stockpile oil, but he could do nothing about the gas.

He had a novel idea but needed to check with a mechanic to see if his idea could work. He received three different opinions and all three mechanics agreed that they could set the car engines to run on kerosene. The vehicles would have an external black exhaust but there would be no damage to the engines.

Felix bought three one hundred gallon drums and a small hand pump and put them in the back yard. Every week he would purchase fifteen to twenty gallons of kerosene and pour it into the drums. He had devised a way to keep his taxis running in case there was a shortage of gasoline.

When asked about his excessive purchase of kerosene, he would simply reply that he had his reasons. The year of 1941 brought hardship to many people all over the world as families were disrupted as many husbands and sons went off to war. Felix was fortunate his car service continued to do well. Early the following year, three more cars were added to his business.

Holiday Season Transportation

There was much preparation on the island for the Christmas holidays. Houses were painted. New furniture was bought, or old pieces were repaired or re-upholstered. Lights and decorations were strung in the streets, in businesses, and on houses. A large part of tradition was the singing of Christmas Carols and musical concerts at the lighting of the big Christmas tree in the Emancipation Garden. Many of the churches placed their Nativity scenes outside of the church.

With all the activity and various Holiday balls to attend throughout the island, the phone at the taxi station was ringing off the hook. Everyone tried to call for car service reservations. The taxi service pickups were for all hours of the day and night. As the number of reservations increased, Felix encouraged couples and friends to share a taxi that would assist him in meeting the needs of more people. The last two weeks of the year would be very profitable for all of his drivers.

The week before Christmas went well. The schedule was working for everyone. He was really proud of the work all the drivers had done throughout the year and he let them know that he appreciated it. As he was fixing the holiday schedule, he remembered that he had to give himself some time off on Christmas Eve night because it was Huldah's birthday.

He rescheduled his calls for that evening to other drivers. He had planned to take Huldah to church for midnight mass on Christmas Eve. They had agreed to attend services at his Catholic Church instead of going to the services at her Anglican Church.

Christmas Eve morning Felix was up early as usual. Huldah was up to make his breakfast. He gave her a hug and a kiss and wished her a Happy Birthday. He ate breakfast and on the way out the door, he stopped to remind her about church that evening. By the time he arrived to the station, a few of the drivers were already there and writing down their schedule from their index cards.

As part of his morning ritual, he would wish his parents and drivers a good morning as he took his pail of water and Chamois skin from the kitchen to clean his car. By the time Felix was finished with his car, the rest of the drivers had arrived, and the phone started to ring.

Within fifteen minutes, all cars were out on assignments. Usually during the holiday season, cars would be on fifteen to thirty minutes turnaround time schedules.

A few of the drivers would come in and take two or three assignments at a time if jobs were in close proximity. Felix had initiated this system to back up drivers who were delayed with assignments or had previous reservations on the board.

On Christmas Eve, Felix arrived home early. Huldah had a meal ready for him. They chatted about their respective day and then got ready for church. Felix's sister sang in the choir and he wanted to arrive early in order to get a seat and to hear the musical selections and Christmas Carols before the Mass began.

When they arrived, Felix stopped on the church steps and kissed Huldah as he again wished her Happy Birthday and Merry Christmas. He told her that she would find her present at home under the mirror on her dresser.

Huldah enjoyed her evening out. She felt blessed that she had someone so special in her life. When they arrived home, she immediately looked under the mirror. There was a fifty-dollar bill and a note, "Stop making your own clothes. Order them from the catalogue."

She smiled and thanked Felix. He was up early the next day and at the station by seven o'clock in the morning. He checked reservations for the day and adjusted reservations for the coming week and New Year's Eve. The year was about to come to an end and all was well with the Silver Streak Taxi Services.

New Business for Silver Streak Taxi Service

Bluebeard's Castle Hotel

The Managers of Bluebeard's Castle Hotel called Felix and invited him to the hotel to talk about the transportation needs of hotel guests. An appointment for the next day was set for one o'clock in the afternoon. The meeting went well. Managers wanted him to maintain two cars at the hotel and to have daily shuttle service to Magens Bay Beach.

Felix agreed to the terms but in turn requested a written contract giving Silver Streak Taxi Service the sole rights to transport guests from their hotel for the duration of three years. Management agreed to Felix's terms and would have a contract ready for his signature in a few days. Felix agreed to begin taxi service within ten days after the contract was signed.

Previously, Felix was also providing taxi shuttle service for employees of the Caribbean Beach Hotel. He decided to ask management for the same request made with the managers of Bluebeard's Castle to station his taxis on site and to include shuttle service to Magens Bay Beach. The manager thought it was a great idea. No longer did guests have to wait for a taxi to come to the hotel to pick them up.

Silver Streak Taxis stationed at the hotel would make travel much easier for guests since the hotel was at the far end of the island closer to the airport. The manager arranged to have three outdoor spaces painted for Silver Streak Taxi Service. Service began ten days after the designated spaces had been painted. Felix provided daily runs to Magens Bay leaving at 10:00 am and returning at 3:00 pm.

Although Felix was happy with the new business arrangement, he was anxious about the fact that he would need additional cars and drivers. Without additional cars and drivers, his prompt service could be compromised. It was time to empty one of his Bibles and arrange for securing funds to purchase additional cars.

The Big Game

When Felix returned to the station, there was a message for him to call Doc who was one of his gambling partners. Before he called Doc, he gathered the drivers to explain the new business ventures with the hotels. He told them about the need for additional cars and drivers.

As was the custom, senior drivers would be assigned the new cars. He asked for their assistance and cooperation during the orientation, preparation, transition, and driver selection. There would possibly be a need for some changes in driver assignments and shifts.

When he called, Doc told him that he was inviting him to a big game on Friday night and the entrance fee would be eight-hundred dollars. Felix replied that he would attend. The big game was supposed to be a well-kept secret, but by that Friday, it was all over town. For the most part, the details concerning the results of the big game were to be kept hush-hush too. However, by the middle of the next day, everybody knew the big winner was Felix. He won over eight thousand dollars in that game.

One of the losers of the game had given Felix an I.O.U. for twelve hundred dollars. This indebted fellow came to the station the next day to settle his gaming loss. As he gave Felix the money, he also referenced that the amount was more than he had originally owed in appreciation of his trust to be paid the following day after the game. The drivers present never forgot the way this debt was repaid. The man had several coin denominations within a large biscuit tin can.

On the island, these tin cans would previously be used to contain saltine crackers, coal, bread, or even water. Sometimes these cans were also painted bright colors and used as planters. This particular biscuit pan had fifty-cent pieces, quarters, dimes, and nickels. It was indeed a group effort to count all the change but the debt amount was accurate with an additional fifty dollars. The Grace of God and Lady Luck had smiled upon Felix and the contents of his Bible remained intact.

Preparing for
New Business Ventures

Felix had much to do in a short period. He had arranged for the purchase of four cars from Mr. Creque, the Chevrolet Dealer. Felix made a list of things he needed to do. He had to go to the cable office to contact the office in Puerto Rico to order roof signs and radios and contact Mr. Hatchet to paint taxi logos on the new cars. He also needed to hire four additional drivers.

As he was finalizing his list, two potential job applicants came to the station. Felix informed the men that a driver would be with them shortly to take them on a driver's test. Selections of applicants were not only based on their successful driver's skills, but also on personal interviews, recommendations, appearance, and communication skills.

Felix informed the applicants that if they did well on the test, he would talk with them about their duties, responsibilities, dress code, schedules, salary, island history, and historical sites to enhance their success as tour guides.

Keeping the Business Running

The beach shuttle was very successful from both hotels. It was as if the guests were just waiting for this type of service. Soon the sightseeing tour business increased. Felix had placed a large sign in each hotel lobby detailing taxi services. Even with his success, Felix was anxious about the impact World War II would have on the tourist industry as well as the supply of gas and oil. He began to avoid any high dollar expenditures and unnecessary spending.

Felix had a maintenance agreement for taxi vehicles with Chief's Garage, which was located by Market Square. The garage took care of mechanical problems; oil changes every twenty- five hundred miles, auto body concerns, and fender repairs. Felix did not have any of his cars driven around with dents and scratches. If the driver was found at fault for any damage to the vehicle, he was required to pay for half of the cost of the repair.

The involvement of the United States in World War II did affect the tourist industry, as well as gas and oil supplies. Felix was pleased that he had had the foresight to stockpile filters, tires, and kerosene oil for his cars. The gas stations informed the public that gas would be rationed. Felix told his drivers about his plan to use kerosene oil if the gas shortage became critical. He assured them that Silver Streak Taxies would continue to operate despite a gas shortage.

Impending Visit From the Stork

Felix and Huldah were married on June 11, 1955. They lived just around the corner from Chief's Garage. He walked home and greeted Huldah who was ironing clothes. She was surprised that he was home so early. He explained to her that he had left his car at Chief's Garage and came home while the oil was being changed.

She fixed him a sandwich and sat with him while he ate. She then told him that she had some news to share. He was going to be a father! He stopped eating and looked up at her. She had a big smile on her face. He jumped up from the table, hugged her tight, kissed her, and said, "Thank you Lord." He asked her if she was sure. Huldah had talked with a midwife. The midwife advised her to see a physician to be sure.

When he arrived back to the station, Felix wasted no time in making an appointment with Dr. Roy Anduze for the following day at 2:00 pm. Felix and Huldah both agreed that they should wait until after the visit with the doctor before telling anyone their good news.

The following day Huldah had her exam and blood tests. The doctor told them that she seemed to be in very good health and to return to the office in three days. They were very anxious on the day of the return visit to the doctor's office. They did not sit too long before Huldah was called into the examination room. Felix sat in the waiting room flipping through pages of magazines. Finally, Dr.

Anduze called him into the examination room. He said, “Congratulations! You are going to be a father.” Felix said, “Thank you, sir” and turned to Huldah smiling.

Dr. Anduze gave Huldah a prescription and an appointment to return in four weeks. They both were bursting at the seams to let everyone know the good news. He drove Huldah to her aunt’s house. Her aunt would be the first to hear their good news. He then went to his parents’ home. Everyone was happy for them. When he returned to the station, he related the baby news to the drivers. He was as proud as a peacock and decided that the following Sunday, he and his wife would attend church together.

Cruise Ships Endorsement of Passenger Prepaid Coupons

In March of 1942, things started looking up for Felix. He found out that he was to be a father and his taxi service business was doing well. With the two hotels onboard the sightseeing business became more important to Silver Streak Taxi Services.

Felix had to find a way to incorporate the sightseeing tour business into the schedules of his shuttle and taxi service, as well ensure his excellent customer service. At the front desk of each hotel were sign-up sheets for beach and sightseeing tours. The front desk clerk at both hotels called the station every morning to state the number of guests for beach trip and the sightseeing tour.

To insure the cooperation of front desk clerks, Felix presented them with an envelope that contained a tip each week. Gradually, both the number of beach trips and sightseeing tours increased.

Tourists were visiting St. Thomas in large numbers despite the fact that the war was still raging in Europe. By summertime, there were one or two cruise ships docked in St. Thomas every week. Many passengers from the ships visited Bluebeard's Castle Hotel. They saw the two signs in the hotel lobby regarding daily beach trips and sightseeing tours. Tourists signed up for one or the other.

Felix asked one of the couples on one of his tours how they had heard of his service. When he learned that it was from the sign in the hotel lobby, it gave him another idea. How could he have passengers on cruise ships sign up for beach trips or island tours prior to the docking of the ship in St. Thomas? Felix thought about it long and hard and the next week he received a visitor's pass to go aboard the cruise ship. He asked one of the staff members to direct him to the person on ship who arranged on-shore sightseeing tours.

Felix was able to talk with the appropriate person. He was told to send his proposal to Southerland Tours. He was given the company name, address and an outline of the information he was required to submit for his proposal. He was also informed that cruise passengers had pre-purchased coupons for activities on shore and these services were paid monthly to the supplier. Felix was thankful for this additional information and promised to return.

When his sister, Elise, arrived home from work he told her about his idea to do business with passengers from the cruise ships. He showed her the information he had obtained from his visit on board the ship. He asked her to prepare a letter to Southerland Tours stating his desire to explore the possibility to provide sightseeing tours and trips to the beach for passengers upon their arrival. He included tentative time schedules for departures and return trips to the ship as well as other proposed costs. Felix was so anxious to receive a response. If he received approval for this new venture, it would do so much for his expanding business.

In a few weeks, Felix received a positive response and contract from Southerland Tours. The company liked the idea of selling both beach trips and sightseeing tours on board ship prior to docking. Passengers who purchased trips or tours would present a prepaid coupon for the appropriate service. These coupons would be submitted to Southerland Tours every month and Felix would be compensated based on the number and type of coupons submitted.

In July 1942, Felix received a list of dates and time cruise ships were scheduled to dock at the port in St. Thomas. On the mornings when ships docked, Felix received a list of passengers with reservations for beach trips and sightseeing tours. In the beginning of this venture, he was able to accommodate the number of reservations with cars from his own fleet.

As the number of cruise ships docked weekly and the number of reservations increased, there were times when he had to utilize trusted drivers who owned private taxis. These drivers would collect the coupons and give them to Felix. He would pay these drivers for the number of trips or tours and submit the coupons at the end of the month to Southerland Tours.

All the drivers did well in the collection of the coupons because that was the only way they were able to get paid for their tours. At the station, each driver had to submit the coupon number and document stating what it was for on his personal index card. Coupons and index cards were placed in a designated box on the desk next to the office phone. This box was also used for all gas receipts for Silver Streak Taxis. Every evening Felix collected and reviewed these cards from the box.

The first month went by quickly. All coupons for the month were mailed to Southerland Tours for payment. Two weeks later Felix received his first check. It was a great feeling. He was so proud that he was able to secure this business venture using the postal system.

Creating a New Business Enterprise With Travel Agencies

One day Felix was standing in the lobby at Bluebeard's Castle Hotel waiting to collect his check for transporting hotel employees. He noticed a guest checking out of the hotel. The man gave the clerk a book of coupons. The clerk removed some coupons, asked the man to sign them, and then gave him a receipt. After the guest left, Felix collected his check from the clerk and asked her about the system of paying with coupons.

She explained that this arrangement was made with travel agencies. Guests arranged trips with a travel agency and received coupons to be presented for airfare and hotel stays. Felix asked her if any of the coupons were from Southerland Tours. She said some guests from Southerland Tours had checked out that day.

Driving back to the station, Felix was thinking about approaching Southerland Tours with the idea of including prepaid coupons for transportation to and from the airport and sightseeing tours. Again, he asked his sister, Elise, to prepare and send a letter to Southerland Tours explaining his newest proposal.

Felix also asked one of the managers at Bluebeard's Castle Hotel for the names of other travel agencies using the coupon system. The manager gave him the name of three agencies: Tropic

Tours, Caribbean Tours, and Puerto Rico Tours. The manager even offered his name to be used as a reference.

Elise sent letters of introduction, proposals for airport transportation and sightseeing tours to the three travel companies. Felix knew that if he were to become successful in securing this additional business, he would have to hire someone to be stationed at the airport to greet guests, collect their luggage, and escort them to the Silver Streak Taxi site.

Silver Streak Taxi Service Establishes a Great Working Environment

Business was moving along in the right direction. The volume of tourist business, shuttle service, and taxi service continued to increase. A barometer of success in the taxi business was the drivers. They all appeared to be pleased with their jobs and there was little driver turnover. It was turning into a family-like environment where they looked out for each other. Drivers were able to submit the names of family members or friends who they thought would be good candidates for Silver Streak employment as positions became available.

The word was out that if you worked for Silver Streak, "Skip," Felix's nickname, took care of you. You were paid every Friday. You had a vehicle at your disposal. You paid for gas for your personal use of the vehicle and always kept the car clean and washed. In addition, if you worked for Silver Streak Taxi Service in any non-driving capacity, such as at the airport to greet arriving guests, you were provided transportation to and from the job site.

It was not until the first week in October that Felix received correspondence from the travel agencies. Tropic Tours was the first to respond to his letter. They liked the idea of adding the options of prepaid coupons for airport transportation and sightseeing tours to the travel package. A form was included within the letter, which Felix was required to complete and return to the company if he wished to pursue this venture. It would be another couple of weeks to get everything in order to begin coupon service.

The second response was from Caribbean Tours. They also expressed a desire to offer options for prepaid coupons for airport transportation and sightseeing tours with their tour packages. The paperwork to be completed and the time frame for a starting date were similar to Tropic Tours. Since he would have prior knowledge of when guests were scheduled to arrive, Felix could have someone to greet the guests and have a car available.

When Felix returned to the station, he had a message to go to the cable office. He had a message to call the manager of Puerto Rico Tours. Felix called and spoke with Mr. Wilson who acknowledged receipt of his letter. Mr. Wilson wanted Felix to come to Puerto Rico to discuss further details of his business endeavor. Felix thanked him for his interest and assured him that he would be happy to come to Puerto Rico.

However, he told Mr. Wilson that he needed some time to plan this trip. He told him about the imminent birth of his first child. He also was thinking that he needed to be available to prepare for the impending busy holiday season. Mr. Wilson agreed to meeting with Felix when he was available and looked forward to hearing from him soon.

Fatherhood and Preparation for Holiday Season

Huldah was moving very slowly as baby delivery time was approaching. Felix discussed with his wife that it might be a good idea for her to stay at her aunt's house during the daytime while he worked until the baby came. He would feel much better at work knowing that she was not alone and was safe. Huldah assured him that she would be fine, but followed his suggestion.

This daylight arrangement only lasted for three days. On November 10, 1942, their first born, a son, Felix Jr., came into the world, with all his fingers and toes in the right place. Huldah was so thankful that the Lord had given them both a healthy baby boy. She said that when Felix saw the baby for the first time, he became all red in the face. He was a proud father and let everyone know. To add to the joy of the day, the wife of his brother, Hidalgo, gave birth to a baby girl a few hours after arrival of his son.

Felix began to learn the new responsibilities of fatherhood; holding a newborn, changing diapers, and middle of the night feedings. Huldah was feeling much better after the delivery and early days of motherhood. Felix told her that he needed to go to Puerto Rico to meet with Mr. Wilson about his newest venture of managing tourists with prepaid coupons. He asked her what she thought about going with him so that her mother, who also lived in

Puerto Rico, could see her new grandson. Huldah liked the idea and thought that it would be a wonderful time to visit her mother.

The busy holiday season was at hand. There were many schedules to be prepared for drivers to accommodate the number of reservations. In the midst of these preparations, he received letters from the two travel agencies with lists of arriving tourists with coupons for airport transportation and/or sightseeing tours. He had to get busy training someone to be at the airport to greet the arriving guests.

The Christmas and New Year of 1942 was great. This was the first Christmas with the new baby and business was booming. All the drivers did well monetarily. Felix hoped that despite the economic effects of the war that the diversity of his business would keep him financially in the black. The baby was putting on weight and doing well. Huldah was also doing well physically. She had adjusted well to her new role as a mother. They took the baby by his parents often and they were always happy to see the baby.

Huldah wrote a letter to her mother to let her know about their upcoming trip instead of arriving as a surprise. She soon received a reply saying that all was well with her mother and her sisters. Her family was anxious to see her and the new baby. Felix was now ready to make an appointment to visit with the manager of Puerto Rico Tours. He called Mr. Wilson and set up a date to meet in Puerto Rico.

Traveling With the Family to Puerto Rico

On the way to the airport, Huldah asked if it was too late to change her mind. "It's too late. You're on the way," replied Felix. This was the first plane ride for either one of them. The baby enjoyed the ride to the airport and Felix held the baby as they boarded the plane. After they boarded, Huldah sat in the aisle seat while Felix and the baby were by the window. She buckled her seatbelt, held on to Felix's arm tightly as she closed her eyes. Meanwhile, the baby and his father had a great time for the thirty-five minutes up in the air to Puerto Rico.

On arrival, as Huldah walked off the plane, she looked up to the sky and said "Thank you Lord." Felix retrieved their luggage and walked out to the taxicab stand. On entering the cab, he gave the driver her mother's address. The driver spoke English very well and told them he knew exactly where the address was located. Felix looked over the interior of the cab checking to see if there was anything he could take back to add to his own car service.

Sporadically, over the taxi radio, a voice could be heard giving verbal driving directions in Spanish to the driver. Felix had asked the driver who was speaking and the driver told him it was the radio dispatcher sending drivers on taxi calls. Felix thought to himself that a radio with a dispatcher would be an asset for his business too.

It did not take too long before the driver arrived at that their destination. By the time Huldah got out of the cab, they heard a loud shriek. “There she is. That is she. That is her.” Her family came running down from the second floor balcony and in no time, they were at the door of the cab. Everybody introduced himself or herself. Elisa Goodridge, Huldah’s mother, greeted Felix and told him how pleased she was to meet him. She insisted that he call her Lisa. Huldah’s sisters, Elma and Vera, did the same and everyone went upstairs to the apartment.

Huldah’s mother was pleased with her grandson, Felix Jr. She kept him in her lap for most of their visit. Felix knew that he would need to get a cab to take them to a hotel that was close to where his meeting would be the next day. Lisa told him one of her neighbors had a cab that would be available in thirty minutes. She would get him to take them wherever they needed to go.

As Huldah’s sisters conversed with Felix, Huldah, the baby, and Lisa were over in another corner catching up on what they had missed for several years that they had not seen each other.

The neighbor who owned the taxi, Raul, finally came home and Lisa brought him over to her house to meet Felix. Felix showed him the address where he had to be the next day. He asked Raul if he could take them to a hotel close to where his meeting was scheduled for the next day. He told Felix that he would take him to a nice hotel close to that address. Felix told Lisa he had to go to a meeting the next day, but that he would arrange for Huldah and the baby to spend time with her.

On the way to the hotel, Felix asked Raul what it would cost to hire him for the day. They agreed on a price. They arrived at the hotel and it was a nice looking place. The plan for the next day was that Raul would pick them up at the hotel, take Felix to his meeting, then take Huldah and the baby to Lisa's house. Felix told the driver what time to pick them up in the morning.

Felix checked them into the hotel and asked the clerk about restaurants that were in the area. The clerk recommended a restaurant located on the left of the hotel lobby. Felix thanked the clerk and the bellhop helped with their luggage to the room. Felix was impressed with the hotel room overlooking the plaza below. There was a king size bed and the bathroom was big with plenty of room.

Huldah fed the baby and while doing so, she told Felix how she enjoyed conversing with her mother and sisters after such a long time. She thought it was going to be difficult, but after seeing them, it was easy to help overcome her anxiousness. They cleaned up, got dressed, and went down for dinner. It was indeed an experience for Felix, as he did not frequent restaurants very often while at home in St. Thomas. They both enjoyed the food and the service. After dinner, they went back to the room. Huldah and the baby were very tired and went to bed. Felix jotted down notes in preparation for his meeting in the morning.

They were up early the next morning. They went to breakfast and took their time because the taxi was not expected for at least an hour and a half. When the taxi arrived, Felix offered Raul breakfast, but he said he had already had breakfast and that he would be outside waiting whenever they were ready. In the taxi, Felix asked the driver to take him to his meeting first and then take Huldah and the baby to Lisa's address.

Embarking on a New Project with Puerto Rico Tours

As Felix entered the office building in Puerto Rico, he noticed how luxurious it was. There was a man in uniform at a desk who asked him which office he sought. Felix told him the office number and the man in the uniform directed him to the elevator on the right for the fourth floor. After Felix exited the elevator, he gave the receptionist his name. The secretary told him to have a seat and she would notify Mr. Wilson of his arrival.

A few minutes later, a tall, blond haired man came out and introduced himself, "Felix Vialet, my name is Charles Wilson. It is great meeting you after all of our phone calls." Felix replied, "I am very glad that you understood my situation and allowed me reschedule our meeting." Mr. Wilson escorted Felix into the conference room and introduced him to the other participants. They met in the conference room for approximately two hours discussing details of the proposed contract. When the meeting was over, Felix came out of the room with his largest contract since beginning his tourist coupon endeavors.

Puerto Rico Tours worked with a majority of the travel agencies on the mainland and the island. Silver Streak Taxi Service was going to be handling all of their tourist arrivals, departures, sightseeing tours, and beach trips on St. Thomas. Puerto Rico Tours handled eighty-five percent of the reservations that came into St. Thomas so that translated into additional work for his company. Felix was extremely pleased when he signed the contract.

Felix could hardly contain himself as he took a taxi back to Lisa's house. He could hardly wait to share his good news with Huldah and her family. Later Felix asked the neighbor next door to take him to the place where he had previously purchased roof signs for his taxis. He needed to get additional signs and was interested in researching the radio dispatcher system he had seen at the airport upon his arrival.

Huldah asked if she and Lisa could go along for the ride. She would leave the baby to spend more time with his aunties. Felix agreed that this would be an opportunity to see parts of the city in Puerto Rico. Lisa was fluent in Spanish and it was a good idea to have her along in case a translator was needed. As they drove along, Lisa pointed out places of interest.

When they arrived at the sign business, Felix told the man that he wanted to purchase additional taxi signs and wanted further information on two-way radio systems for his taxis. The man said he had just the person to help him with all radio concerns. The man returned with an older man and told Felix, "This is the radio man, but he doesn't speak much English. Tell me what you need and I will tell him. We will see if he can build a radio system to meet your needs." The three-way conversation went on for a while.

The older man told Felix that he could build a radio setup that would work from downtown to the east end of the island, but he was not sure how much reception he would get on the west end of the island due the number of high hills in St. Thomas. He also told Felix that he would need to erect an antenna at least the height of a telephone pole. Felix asked the man to send a detailed list of what he needed to do to get the system up and working when he shipped him the completed taxi signs.

It was now past lunchtime. Felix suggested that they stop to get something to eat. Lisa told him that she had prepared something and would like them to eat at her house. She also told him that the driver's wife would be upset if he too was late for his lunch meal. The driver smiled and thanked Lisa in Spanish. Felix enjoyed Lisa's cooking. With no air conditioning in the house, it was cooler to sit out on the balcony after lunch. He wanted to give Huldah and her family as much time together as possible since they were to return to St. Thomas the following morning.

While Felix was on the balcony, the taxi driver returned to ask if they were ready to go back to the hotel. Felix went inside to let Huldah know it was time to go. She gathered up the baby's things and said her goodbyes. Felix shook hands with everyone and told them how pleased he was to have met them. He promised to have Huldah visit more often. Huldah was quite sad during the ride back to the hotel.

The next morning, the taxi driver picked them up and took them to the airport. Felix thanked him for all he had done and paid him. He told him he hoped to have the same arrangement whenever he returned to Puerto Rico. Huldah gave the driver a hug and asked him to continue to look out for her family. They checked in at the airline and in approximately forty-five minutes, they were boarding the plane for home.

Preparing for New Business

They were up early the next day as usual. Huldah fixed Felix's breakfast. He teasingly turned to her and said, "I was getting use to the idea of going downstairs in the hotel for breakfast." Huldah returned with a smile, "You had better remember it was like this before the hotel." It was going to be a very busy day for him.

When he arrived to the station, he pushed the gate and the bell rang. For a moment, he stopped to think about his dog, Teddy. This was where his dog used to greet him and now that he had passed, Felix was thinking it was time to get a new watchdog.

He said good morning to everyone and asked his sister if she would be ready to go to work soon. She asked how things went in Puerto Rico. Felix told her he would fill her in on the way to work. On the drive to work, he told her about his meetings and about the contract he attained. He told her about meeting Huldah's mother and sisters. He thought that everyone enjoyed the visit.

By the time, he returned from taking his sister to work, most of the drivers were in the station. Some were already out on their early morning reservations. Felix shared the news about the new contract with the drivers present. He let them know that he would be hiring two drivers and two greeters to accommodate the new business expansion. As usual he encouraged them to submit names of people they wished to recommend.

Felix wanted to be prepared for the new business generated by the contract with Puerto Rico Tours. He needed to have greeters at the various hotels and at the airport. He negotiated with hotel and airport managements to have booths placed in very visible locations in the hotel lobby and in the airport. He had telephones installed in each of the booths. He had his friend Mr. Hatchet paint the Silver Streak Taxi logo painted on the booths.

Felix also secured four parking spaces for Silver Streak vehicles in the airport terminal. These cabs transported only the guests arriving with coupons for Silver Streak transportation. They did not transport any other passengers, thus avoiding competition for business with other taxi drivers.

The business from Puerto Rico Tours started in March of 1943 with five reservations in the mail for transportation and sightseeing tours. The business steadily increased. Business at Silver Streak Taxi was fantastic. The morale of the employees was high as they started to enjoy the increase in their weekly pay. Felix was pleased with his accomplishments. Felix lost some of his drivers who had to fulfill military obligations.

The word spread quickly that Silver Streak Taxi Service was hiring drivers and he was able to get qualified replacement drivers. The ongoing war left a cloud of uncertainty about the tourist industry. Felix was aware of the importance of continuing to provide the best service ever to his local clientele. The coupon business could fluctuate but the local business was steady.

Transportation Arrangements With Sailors on Navy Ships and Submarines

Navy ships also stopped in St. Thomas and sailors were given leave for one or two days. They needed taxis to go everywhere on the island and to the beach. They had heard about Magens Bay and everyone wanted to go there. Felix allowed the drivers to transport sailors after they had completed their workday with Silver Streak as long as they provided their own gas.

The sailors brought quite a bit of revenue to the island during those two short days. The sailors were eager to blow off some steam. Liquor was cheap and plentiful. Not surprisingly, local and military law enforcement personnel were quite busy during these two days.

Although there was a war going on, the Caribbean remained a popular destination for travel. Cuba, Puerto Rico, and the Virgin Islands were the most popular vacation sites. The growth of tourism in St. Thomas resulted in improvements to the infrastructure as well as new construction of homes and hotels. Predictions for future growth were encouraging.

Felix thought his business was in a very good position to do well. The Christmas season was coming up and he needed to start plans to accommodate the holiday rush of business along with the new business ventures that he had initiated. Local reservations for the holidays had doubled last year so it would be a greater challenge to plan.

Felix's sister, Elise who was not a driver, was the most valuable component to Silver Streak Taxi Service. She kept the business books in order. She made deposits, prepared payroll, and paid the bills. She sent out the completed coupon vouchers to the travel agencies for collection and billed for the employee shuttle services. Felix was confident that this aspect of his business was in good hands.

The next group of employees who were not drivers was the greeters who worked in the hotels and at the airport. The airport greeters were important because they were the first person to greet arriving guests. That individual had to be polite and knowledgeable of the various accommodations offered by each travel agency. The employees he had assigned to the airport did a first class job. Felix let them know that everybody was depending on them to make all guests comfortable and they assisted in making all jobs easier.

The greeters at the hotel were equally important because they interacted with the guest throughout their entire stay on the island. They helped to setup tours, beach trips, restaurant reservations, and nightlife. There was now a greeter at Blue Beard's Castle Hotel, Caribbean Beach Hotel, Flamboyant Hotel, Villa Olga Hotel, and Gramboco Hotel.

Island Taxi Competition and Diversification of Silver Streak Taxi Services

Silver Streak Taxi Service had started a new way of making a living in St. Thomas. Other taxi stands also started to spring up all over the island. At first Felix thought it would hurt his business, but for some strange reason it made things better. Competition made drivers provide better customer service; and in turn, that helped the drivers retain customers.

Those satisfied customers would recommend others. The sprouting new cab companies consisted primarily of individual cab owners who congregated in one central area with a telephone. As these independent cabs lined up, they were dispatched according to their line placement. Most taxi owners owned only one car.

Felix's goal was to diversify his business so that he was not dependent only on the phone to ring for taxi service to make a living. As the tourist business grew, the need for accommodations grew along with it. More hotels and guesthouses were built. Felix saw these as potential sites for additional business.

Before a new hotel or guesthouse was completed, Felix tried to make his services known to management. He sought contracts to transport their employees back and forth to work. He also explored the possibility of having a booth in the lobby to offer sightseeing tours and beach trips. Later he made a bid to station one taxi at each new hotel.

The month of January started out with a bang. Coupon reservations began very high for the first two weeks of the month. If the rest of the month kept up at this rate, it would be the best month since Felix started with transportation coupons. By the last week in the month, he received coupon reservations from Puerto Rico Tours.

It started with sixteen for that coming month and the following week he received the reservations for the rest of the month. The work was there. All he had to do was to make sure that all his employees provided and continued their excellent customer service. Customer satisfaction would create more business.

Back to Garden Street and the Second Move for the Family

Felix had heard that a neighbor of his parents was moving. He inquired if the apartment was available for rent. Late that afternoon, after finishing his runs, he found a note left at the station. The apartment was available for rent. Felix was happy with this information.

This meant that he could move into a larger place. The apartment had three bedrooms, an eat-in kitchen, and a small parlor. He thought that Huldah would love the new apartment. He decided to take care of the details to rent the apartment and then surprise Huldah with the news. Felix went to the landlady's home and completed the arrangements. He was so happy to move into a larger home, which was close to his family and his place of business.

When Felix arrived home, he gave Huldah the news. She was so happy and exclaimed, "Thank you Lord." She wanted to know how soon they could move. He said, "I will take you there tomorrow morning so that you can see it and decide what needs to be done before I hire a truck."

The next morning Huldah was up before the baby. Too excited to sleep, she started the day a bit early. She wanted to see the new apartment as soon as possible. This was going to be a big step up for her because she had never lived in an apartment with more than three rooms and now she was going to have one of her own with more than six rooms. She gave Felix his breakfast, and then fed and bathed the baby. Felix played with his son while she got ready to view the new apartment.

Their new apartment had two windows and two doors on the street side and one window on the side facing Miss Pickwood, the next-door neighbor's walkway. The apartment was clean. The former tenants had left some furniture that included a bed mattress, and one small dresser in one bedroom and two small tables in the parlor room.

Huldah walked around the apartment as if she was trying to decide where she would place furniture. Felix stood in one corner just looking at her for a few minutes. She walked over to him and asked if they had funds to get additional furnishings. Felix agreed to buy the things she wanted.

Before she had met Felix, she had started saving dishes, pots, and pans for her own place. She could not believe that it would ever happen like this -- a husband, a family, and now her own large three-bedroom apartment.

She gave Felix a long hug. They walked down the hill to his mother's house and visited there for a while. When she arrived back home, Huldah was giddy with the anticipation about moving. She gathered up the baby and walked over to give her Aunt and cousins the good news.

The following morning in-between taxi runs, Felix drove down past the market square looking for the delivery truck driver who had previously moved him into his present apartment. Felix left a message for the truck driver to contact him. The next day the truck driver came by the station. He and Felix agreed on a date and time to move the furniture and household items from the old apartment. The move went smoothly. Felix and his family were settled into their new place quickly. The timing was perfect. Felix soon learned that there would be another new addition to his family.

Perks of Living Near the Job and Poker Games

With the new apartment, Felix was now so close to his business that he could stay late or return later to create driver schedules without any interruptions. Although his business still had peaks and valleys, he started to do very well. He gradually was able to decrease the number of runs that he did personally and devote more time to managing the business.

Soon after the move, Felix received a call from one of his card-playing friends inviting him to a game that coming weekend. Felix agreed to attend. His friend told him where and what time it would be on Thursday, Friday and Saturday nights. There was a five-hundred-dollar entrance fee and five players were going to be there.

That Thursday, Felix played cards until two o'clock in the morning and lost. He had a better night on Friday night. He won back what he lost the night before plus five hundred dollars. That Saturday night, he won close to three thousand dollars. When he left the game that night, he said to himself that he would invest the money he won into buying an antenna for his taxi radio system.

He had already received the price list for all the parts for the radio-dispatcher system. It was going to cost a pretty penny to purchase the antenna, base station, and radios for all of the vehicles.

He planned to purchase four additional ones for when he added more vehicles. Felix decided to purchase the antenna first.

On the left side of the station, he already had a small antenna for his short wave radio. He would have to remove it and dig a larger hole to accommodate the larger pole for the radio antenna. The next week, he employed a man to dig a hole for the new pole. The pole had to be large enough to accommodate a power pole. He paid the power company to erect one of their wooden power poles. The antenna would be erected on top. The entire process took about three weeks.

For the next three to four months, things went along smoothly with the exception of a few car fender benders and a few engine repairs. These little mishaps caused a few changes in scheduling and down time for vehicles. With the prevalence of war, a number of auto parts were very hard to obtain. Car batteries were difficult to purchase.

Tar was melted to remove good cells from bad batteries to recreate good ones. Felix sacrificed one of his oldest vehicles for parts to keep his taxi fleet going. When things improved, he would refurbish old vehicles and have them running again.

Brakes were one of the parts that were constantly being changed on the vehicles, because of all the hills on the islands. A driver had to listen to his vehicle for any noise emerging from his brakes. If any noise was heard, the vehicle was immediately stopped to ensure that metal parts of the brake shoes were not damaged further. Since metal parts were hard to get because of the war, other parts could be purchased from the local auto parts store. Having drivers do preventive maintenance avoided costly repairs to his vehicles.

Birth of a Second Child and Third Move for the Family

On November 4, 1944, a daughter was born to Felix and Huldah Vialet and they named her Noreen. She had all of her little fingers and toes. They were proud of the birth of their second child.

With the birth of his second child, Felix had the opportunity to own another business. He was told by his brother about a building nearby with a small bar on the ground floor and a three-bedroom apartment upstairs. Felix considered speaking with the owner about the property. The apartment where he was currently living was on a hill. This property was on level ground. It would be much easier for Huldah to maneuver with two small children.

He thought that even if the rent was slightly higher than what he was currently paying, the proceeds from the bar would offset his additional rent. He called the owner and made an appointment for the next day to look over the property. All day, he thought about what he was about to do to plan for his future. It was less than a year and his family was not yet settled into their current apartment. Felix wondered how Huldah would feel about moving again so soon.

The next day he was anxious about going to see the place, but he kept the appointment. The owner was waiting for him. They started in the upstairs apartment. It was newly painted and was ready to be occupied. They went downstairs to the bar, which was also clean and newly painted. There were glasses, liquor, containers for ice, and other items to operate the bar in the room. Felix liked everything about the property so they sat down and started to discuss price. It did not take long for Felix and the owner to come to an agreement.

The owner explained to Felix that he could only rent the place for a year and a half to possibly two years at most. If he agreed to those terms Felix could rent the building. Felix agreed to the terms and would meet the next day to finalize the transaction.

Felix returned home to tell Huldah about his agreement. She thought it was a good idea, but she had one question for him. “What are you going to do about the bar? You don’t know one thing about running a bar.” Felix replied, “I will have to get someone to operate the bar until I can handle it myself.”

He was concerned about moving again so soon and hoped it would not be bothersome for his wife. Huldah assured him that she was agreeable to the move. The next day, he met with the owner, finalized the transaction, and then move number three was in motion. It took Felix approximately two weeks to get his family moved.

He was able to get his brother and a friend to help out with the bar. People who came to play cards also bought drinks, therefore the bar also made money.

Fulfilling the Dream of Becoming a Boss

Felix wanted to be like his father, in charge of his own destiny and to be his own boss. With the taxi service and now a bar, he was on his way to accomplishing his goals. To find a way to increase what he began and to sustain the business, he had to continue to emphasize to all of his employees the two most important things in business was to be punctual and consistently maintain good customer service. This was a winning recipe for a prosperous business.

Felix hired a full-time employee to answer the phone to dispatch drivers. The dispatcher recorded each call on index cards and taxis were dispatched according to the order in which the calls were received and/or by proximity to the drivers' locations. Each day, different drivers were assigned to be located at the station to respond to in-coming calls. When a driver returned from a call, he would blow his horn twice before parking his taxi, to let the dispatcher know he had returned. This taxi pick-up operation worked very smoothly. On a busy day, each driver handled approximately twenty to twenty-five calls. If business was slow, the men would remove the plywood, which covered the pool table, and play a game of pool until the phones would ring again for taxi service.

Everyone on the island knew that when Silver Streak Taxi Service was called, that they would get a rapid response. Felix listened to people in his cab as they talked about other taxi services. Many complaints concerned the length of time customers had to wait for someone to answer the phone; unavailable drivers; or delay in arrival of cabs.

Upon listening to the people in his taxi, Felix knew that he was on the right track in making his business better than the other taxi services by providing prompt, courteous service. A satisfied customer became an ambassador for his company.

Felix never sat idly when his taxis needed repairs. When cars had fender benders or transmission trouble, he would immediately send vehicles to Chief's Garage for repairs. He took the time to adjust or juggle shifts and schedules to accommodate for vehicles that were out of commission. The drivers without vehicles were assigned to dispatching, greeting hotel guests, or filling in for drivers on their days off. Silver Streak Services was always available for their valued customers.

Installation of Two-Way Radios and Dispatcher System

Things went well for both of his businesses. The downstairs bar did very well over the holidays and things went especially well with the taxi business. All of the drivers did a superb job working with the large number of taxi reservations. A few mix-ups occurred with coupon customers who had changed their travel locations. At times like these, a radio system would come in handy for the taxi business. The goal for Felix was to have a radio system installed this coming year. He could shorten response time to calls and correct mix-ups if he had a radio to direct drivers.

Finally, Felix placed an order with the company in Puerto Rico for a radio system. It consisted of a base system and twenty- four receivers for the cars. The complete package cost about two thousand dollars. He arranged with the Virgin Islands National Bank to send the funds to the company in Puerto Rico. Within a few days, the company sent Felix a telegram confirming receipt of the funds. They were in the process of putting the system together to send to St. Thomas. A technician would come to St. Thomas to install the antenna, base unit, and radios in the vehicles and ensure all was working well.

The company in Puerto Rico took care of the FCC license for Felix. When the radios were installed, the technician had Felix place a vehicle at Red Hook, Black Point Hill, Mountain Top, Magen's

Bay, and Flamboyant Hotel to determine the reception from the office base at the station. In a few locations, the position of the vehicles had to be altered to improve reception.

Other than a few quirks, the radios worked. Felix had elevated his taxi business to the next level. The erection of a radio antenna for the two-way radio system for the taxis had an additional use for the station. The shortwave radios allowed everyone to listen to baseball, boxing, major sports events, and world news.

After approximately two months of driving with the new radios, the drivers approached Felix as a group to thank him for the installation. Everyone could see the increase in revenue. He also thanked employees for their loyalty and service. He stated that he would continue to do anything to make things better for everyone. His expectations were for everyone to work together to make Silver Streak Taxi Service a good place to work.

An End of War, a Birthday Party, Another Addition to the Family, and Giving Thanks

The war was the biggest radio news story. Although there were a number of casualties for American families, the feeling was that the end of the war was nearby. The phone rang jarring Felix from his thoughts. A driver answered it and the caller said, "Turn on your shortwave radio." No sooner was the radio turned on, when the announcer yelled, "The war is over! The war is over!"

It was August 9, 1945, a day that will always be remembered and written in history. Everyone began cheering and hugging each other. All over the world, the same thing must have been happening. Felix silently thanked the Lord for this victory and blessed everyone that lived through this horrific war and prayed for those who did not survive.

By the end of September and the beginning of October, after the end of the war, soldiers returned home to resume their lives. Everyone tried to help the soldiers in any way they could to get them readjusted, especially with employment. Felix had purchased new cars and this was as good a time as any to hire soldiers.

The service men started returning home and Felix was happy to rehire those men who had worked for him prior to their time with the military. One of the men who returned from the service in November was Mr. Thompson, "Tom," a mechanic by trade.

To have a driver with skills as a mechanic onboard would save him repair expenses. Mr. Thompson would be able to reduce the downtime of vehicles in need of minor mechanical repairs. Previously cars would have to sit in a mechanic's shop for several days. A car in a repair shop did not make any money.

November was also the month Felix's two children were born. The oldest, Junior, would be three on the tenth, and the second, Noreen, would celebrate her first birthday on the fourth. His wife had arranged a small party and invited some of their cousins and family members. Junior enjoyed the party very much and he had fun.

Noreen put her hand in the cake and licked her fingers. She liked the sweet icing and enjoyed her presents. Everyone had fun and enjoyed the cake, ice cream and the party favors to take home. It was a wonderful day.

This Thanksgiving will really be special for we have been blessed with many things to be thankful. Grannie prepared a Thanksgiving dinner like no other. There was something for everyone. Most of her children and their families came to partake in the meal. Some of the drivers who did not have any family also ate. It was a very good and blessed Thanksgiving Day.

That day, Huldah gave Felix the news that he was about to become a father for the third time. He was happy to receive the news as with all his children. Felix loved his family and would do everything and anything he could for them. He remembered that he had promised Huldah's mother that she would visit her more frequently. Therefore, he thought that this would be a good time for Huldah to visit her mother so that she could see her grandchildren before the newest arrival.

The next evening when he made the suggestion to Huldah, he was surprised when she stated, "You know I was thinking about the same thing." Felix suggested that she and the children spend the Christmas holidays in Puerto Rico with her family. Huldah liked that idea very much. Felix told her that he would make reservations for them to go to Puerto Rico the second week in December which would give her mother time to prepare for their arrival.

The next day Felix picked up the airline tickets. Huldah immediately sat down and wrote a letter to her mother announcing the news she was expecting her third child and their impending visit during the upcoming holidays.

Although she was excited for the trip to Puerto Rico to visit her mother, it was going to be a bit challenging for Huldah. The first time travelling on the plane was scary even though her husband accompanied her. This time Huldah would have to conquer her fears and be strong for the children as she travelled alone without Felix.

When it was time to depart, she was nervous but she tried to keep her emotions low key as not to scare the children. She walked out to the plane with one child in her arms and one holding her hand. They walked up the stairs to the inside of the plane and disappeared from Felix's vision below. Within fifteen minutes, the plane taxied down the runway.

On his way home, Felix stopped at the station office and then went home to an empty house. He was satisfied to hear that Huldah and the children had arrived safely in Puerto Rico. His house had never been empty since he had been together with Huldah and had children. It was a strange feeling to be alone as Felix went to bed, closed his eyes, and drifted off to sleep.

To keep busy while his family was away, Felix conducted his annual evaluation of each driver by reviewing his index cards. This gave him an idea of how each driver was doing and indicated where the calls were coming from. He also met with each driver to discuss strengths and any areas in need of improvement.

At this time, Felix had stationed Silver Streak Taxis at two hotels, Bluebeard's Castle, and Caribbean Beach Hotel. In review of the cards there were additional calls emanating from Adams Guesthouse, Grand Hotel, 1829 Hotel, Higgins's Gate Guesthouse, Harbor View Guesthouse, Miller's Manor Guesthouse, Flamboyant Hotel, Villa Olga Hotel, Smith's Fancy Guesthouse, Trade Winds Hotel and Club Contant. The drivers were doing well.

Most of the calls appeared to be coming from small guesthouses and hotels. This evaluation review helped him to decide if he should try to station Silver Streak Taxis at additional hotel sites during peak hours.

Felix was happy when his family returned from Puerto Rico. Huldah and the children were happy to return home too. He had missed the ride along he had with his son standing on top of his seat until the motion of the car lulled him to sleep. They spoke of their adventure on the plane and Felix spoke of missing his wife's cooking. Huldah was doing well and the baby was expected in June.

Their third child, Aubrey, was born on June 23, 1946. Huldah and Felix were very happy with the birth of their third child. Huldah's aunt came over to help with the other children while she was in the hospital. As she recuperated at home, they were thankful to have assistance with the newborn and other two children. Although he enjoyed the time with his children, Felix frequently had to return to the station to oversee the growing business.

Death of the Family Patriarch

Felix arrived to the Silver Streak Taxi Station early one morning in December 1946, and pushed open the gate ringing the bell. Over the sound of the bell, he did not hear the usual laughter, but the sound of people crying loudly. He rushed to his mother's front door, which was open. His mother, sister, and cousin were all sobbing. "What is the matter?" Felix asked with urgency in his voice. His sister put her hands from cupping her face and said, "Papa is dead."

Felix stood still for a few minutes to gather himself and then asked to see his father. Elise said, "He is in his room." He did not get up early as usual, so I knocked on the door a few times. When he did not answer, I called Ma. She came and knocked, but there was no answer. She then opened the door. Ma called out Papa's name twice but he did not move. She walked over to the bed and shook him. She silently stood over the bed for a few minutes and then cried out, "Your father is dead." Louis Flavel Vialet was born January 1, 1883 and died December 13, 1946.

Felix approached his father's door that was ajar. He entered and stood next to the bed where his father was lying with his eyes closed as if he were sleep. Felix made the sign of the holy cross as he prayed over the body of his father. Aloud he recited the Lord's Prayer and when he was finished he said, "Bless him Lord. He was a good man, a good father and even with all of our differences, I loved him."

Felix left the room in shock with the passing of his father. He was not sure as to what to do next. He knew the authorities had to be notified in order to receive the death certificate. He needed assistance and knew the person who could help him with the necessary procedures lived up the hill from the house. Felix told his mother that he was going up the hill to get Mr. "Gunney" Maduro.

Felix knocked on the door at the top of the hill. Mrs. Maduro opened the door and Felix asked to see Gunney. "My father has died and I need his help," Felix said sadly. She put her hand over her mouth and softly said, "Oh, Felix, I am so sorry. Please accept my condolences on your loss. I will get Gunney for you right away." She went inside to call her husband. Gunney immediately came to the door and Felix told him the sad news. Gunney agreed to come down the hill to assist the family.

Felix went back down to the house to wait for him. Gunney came into the house and asked to be taken to his father's room. Gunney told Felix that he would assist with preparing the body. He told the family he would retrieve the paperwork to get a burial permit, build a coffin, and help provide transportation for funeral services. These preparations were all necessary at this time because there were no funeral parlors on the island of St. Thomas.

Felix removed the mattress from his father's bed leaving the bedspring in place. Blocks of ice covered with several layers of cruder (burlap) bags were placed on the bedspring. The body of Flavel Vialet was laid atop the bags in his home until the day of his burial. Felix comforted his mother and sister.

Felix went to the station to delegate one of the drivers to be in charge of the taxi business while he took care of his family. He then returned home to tell his wife that his dad had passed. She was sad but supportive and hugged him tight. He could feel her tears running down the side of his face. She liked his father.

Felix informed his wife that he had to take care of a number of items for his family and that he would be a late coming back home that evening. He suggested that if she wanted, she could walk up to his parent's home and give them a hand with things for a while. Huldah said she would go to help.

He left the house to purchase cruder bags and blocks of ice. He bought large blocks of ice and had them cut in half so they would fit into the trunk of his car. The exit from the ice plant was directly across the street from the Catholic Church. He parked his car and entered the church. Again, he said a prayer for his father. When he returned to the house, the neighbors in town had received word of his father's death. His brothers were there comforting their mother as other family members came and went.

Gunney and another man known as "Dollars" were at the house to help with replacing the ice blocks on the bedsprings. A few of the cruder bags were laid under the bed to catch melting ice. Ice had to be purchased every day, cruder bags placed under the bed, and those covering his father had to be wrung out two to three times a day until the day of the funeral.

On the day of the funeral, the family dressed Flavel in his white suit and placed him inside the coffin. All of Felix's brothers and his two sisters came to their father's funeral. He was given a joyous tribute and "Home Going Ceremony" by his children and wife. He was buried in the Western Cemetery on the island of St. Thomas, Virgin Islands.

After the funeral, the brothers and sisters sat down to put a plan in motion to make their mother comfortable. Her husband was her life. His death would leave a void in her daily routine. First thing that had to be done was to make sure that the things that their father had put in place to keep her comfortable were continued. The brothers and sisters decided that each would make a monetary contribution every month to make sure that their mother was well taken care of financially.

Although Hidalgo, Lionel, Rudolph, Elise, Flavel, Audrey, Theodore, and Aubrey all kept in close contact with their mother, Elise, Felix, Susthen, and Lois saw her every day because they lived on the island. Felix had his business at the house property and Elise continued to live at home with her mother. The grandchildren Ulrika, Leonia, Eloise and Elise helped grocery shopping, cleaning, washing, and cooking. Despite all the help from her children and grandchildren, everyone knew Granny was still in charge of the Vialet complex.

The Travel Industry Peaks and the Fourth Move for the Family

Puerto Rico Tours were the largest source of off island business for Silver Streak Services. He also had the tourist coupon business from Tourism International, Southerland Tours, and Virgin Islands Tours. Cruise ships stopped more frequently in St. Thomas. Several travel agencies on the island recommended Silver Streak Taxi Service for the transportation needs of their guests.

On occasion when Felix had more guests than his vehicles could efficiently handle, he called on several reliable and trusted independent taxi drivers to assist. These drivers were able to provide the same quality of service he expected from his own employees.

Travel to the Caribbean soared from 1947 through 1949. As a United States territory, St. Thomas was a popular vacation spot. Silver Streak Services gained much from the established contacts with various travel agencies. Silver Streak was doing very well and Felix's downstairs bar had done well in the two years of ownership.

The property owner's two-year lease on the building would soon expire. Once again, it would be time to look for a new apartment. Felix was sad to give up the lucrative bar. One day on his way up to Bluebeard's Castle Hotel, Felix saw a "For Rent" sign on a building at the bottom of the hill. He stopped to inquire about the apartment. He spoke with the owner who resided at the property. After a short conversation with Felix, the owner decided to rent him the apartment. She agreed to waive the first month's rent if Felix agreed to clean and paint the apartment himself. Felix made the agreement. Move number four was about to take place.

The next day, Felix notified his old landlord that he would be moving. He asked the landlord if he would like to purchase equipment and fixtures he had added to the bar. The landlord agreed to pay Felix for all the additions and furnishings that he had added to the bar. Felix was happy with the deal and told him he would be moving to a new apartment in approximately two weeks.

He then went upstairs to tell his wife about the new apartment. Usually Felix would inform his wife of his plans prior to making a commitment. But he was afraid to lose the deal for the new apartment. He told Huldah all the details concerning the new apartment, information about the owner and assured her that he would take her and the kids to see the new place the next day.

Huldah was content with the two-week arrangement because it would give her time to pack. The next day Felix took his family to meet the landlord and to see the new apartment. Huldah and the owner, Miss Camps, became acquainted and appeared to like one another. There was a porch in the front of the apartment and plenty of yard space for the children to run around outside. The family never had this much space in the previous apartments. There were neighbors in the back of the apartment who also had children of a similar age.

While their children were being acquainted with the neighbor's children, Felix and Huldah looked around the apartment to see what was needed to get the apartment ready for their move. When they were leaving, Huldah saw a section in the front of the porch area where she could plant flowers. This was something she had wanted to do for a long time. With help from his brothers and friends, Felix had the new apartment cleaned, painted, and ready to move into in two weeks.

An Exclusive Business Contract With the Virgin Isle Hotel

New opportunities were on the horizon to further enhance the success of Felix's business. One morning, there was a call at the station for a day trip for two passengers. The caller requested Felix as their driver. Notified of the request, he delegated other drivers to cover his reservations. He left the station and went back home to wash and change his shirt. He drove to the requested pickup site at the local Post Office.

As soon as he parked, he was approached by two gentlemen. They asked if he was Felix and he verified that they were the two guests for the day trip. They introduced themselves as Sidney Kessler and Ben Bayne. When they were comfortably seated, they told Felix that they had requested him as their driver on the recommendation from a previous passenger.

They requested Felix take them to visit places where tourists had not travelled or toured. Felix took them from Botany Bay on the west end of the island to Red Hook on the east end. He took them to the north side and to Flamboyant Hotel on the southeast side. As he drove through the different sections of St. Thomas, he related the history of the island and answered their questions.

On the drive back towards town, Mr. Kessler told Felix that he and Mr. Bayne were the owners of the new Virgin Isle Hotel that was being built on John Dunko Hill. Construction of the one hundred and forty-room hotel was progressing well. Opening day was three to four months away.

They were now making plans for the daily operations of the hotel. They would need twenty-four hour onsite taxis to provide guests with immediate service. The gentlemen wanted to know if Felix thought his business could provide this type of service. He was pleased that his business was being considered and told them that he would be pleased to accept their offer.

An agreement was made to develop a proposal based on their requirements and to submit it the following day. Felix explained that he currently owned twenty-eight cars to handle his current customers' needs. He would need to purchase additional cars to meet the quota of this new business endeavor. Once he had a contract agreement, Felix contemplated that he would use it as collateral for a loan to purchase additional cars.

Felix took Mr. Kessler and Mr. Bayne back to Bluebeard's Castle. The new Virgin Isle Hotel owners had agreed that Felix should leave the proposal at the front desk for Mr. Kessler the next day. When he returned to the station, he immediately began to draft a proposal because he wanted assurance that Silver Streak would be the exclusive provider of taxi service for the newest hotel on the island.

Initially, he requested a four-year contract with the opportunity to renew thereafter. Felix sought additional input from his sister, Elise. She assured him that it was an excellent business enterprise and she would have his proposal typed and ready for him to submit the next day.

The next morning the drivers inquired about Felix's special private tour. This was the first time that someone had requested Felix as a specific driver for a tour. Felix told the drivers who the guests were and the possibility of doing business with the newest hotel. Everyone was excited and certain it would be a blessing.

Elise had the proposal ready as promised. Felix delivered the proposal to the Bluebeard's Castle Hotel. He received a phone call from Mr. Kessler verifying receipt of his proposal. He promised Felix he would have a response in a few days. The following week Felix was invited by the new hotel owners to have lunch at Bluebeard's Castle Hotel to discuss his proposal. The men told Felix that they could meet the terms of his proposal, but they had an additional request to transport their employees to and from work at a reduced rate.

Felix explained that he currently had contracts with three hotels to transport their employees to and from work for a rate of thirty-five cents per person per trip. Employees were picked up at a designated location at a specific time and returned to the same location at a designated time. Felix said that that was the lowest rate that he could offer. They continued the discussion throughout their lunch.

Finally, they agreed to his financial terms. Details of the employee transportation agreement were added as an addendum to the initial proposal. They suggested that Felix have an attorney review the final proposal before submitting it back to them with his signature. Once the contract was prepared, reviewed, signed, and notarized, Felix was able to use the document as collateral to apply for a loan to purchase additional cars for his expanded business.

The same afternoon, Felix waited until most of the drivers had returned to the station before he shared the news about the contract with the new hotel. He told them that he had submitted a proposal to have Silver Streak Taxi Service provide exclusive taxi service for guests and employees at the one-hundred forty-room Virgin Isle Hotel under construction on John Dunko Hill.

If approved, the contract would run for four years with an opportunity to renew. He explained further that this new venture would mean the purchase of new cars and the hiring of additional drivers and greeters to be stationed at the new hotel. Details about assignments of drivers would come later. The drivers were excited at the prospect of additional work and income. They cheered Felix as they expressed gratitude and pride for his newest business venture.

Felix had his sister prepare the employee transportation proposal to the original proposal. He then presented the proposal to his attorney for review. He resubmitted the proposal to the hotel owners. He anxiously awaited notification of approval. When he got word of approval he met with the owners to sign it. With the signed contract, Felix now turned his attention to the purchase of twelve new vehicles.

He made sure that there was enough money on hand for payroll and fuel expenses for one month. He would have to use his personal savings as a down payment and submit the new hotel contract as collateral for a bank loan to purchase the new vehicles. He took the contract to Mr. Lindqvist at the Ford dealership. He explained that to fulfill the contract he needed to purchase twelve additional vehicles. Previously he had purchased cars based on trade-in value of old vehicles and received loans directly from the dealership.

This time he would have to obtain a loan from the bank to finance his deal. Mr. Lindqvist provided documentation verifying terms for the purchase and the amount of money requested. Felix took the documents and the contract to the bank to apply for the loan. Through his reputation as a good businessman, excellent credit, family reputation in the community, recommendation from Mr. Lindqvist, and value of the new contract, Felix was able to secure a loan with satisfactory terms from the bank. He felt blessed that he had so much support for his newest business venture.

The job of hiring drivers and greeters was a time consuming process. Felix trusted his drivers to present worthwhile recommendations. He evaluated each applicant on his driving skills, neat appearance, prior work experience, and ability to interact with customers.

In addition to good people skills, the drivers and greeters needed to have knowledge of the history of the island. It did not take long for word to spread that Silver Streak Taxi Service was hiring. He evaluated those recommended by his drivers first. Within a few weeks, the selected drivers and greeters were hired and new vehicles were ordered.

It was a busy time for Felix. Again he had to order roof signs and radios for the new cars. These vehicles would also need to have logos painted on the doors. Felix was nervous about these expenditures before he actually received any income from the new hotel still under construction. He could hardly wait for the new hotel to ultimately open.

When he was notified that the new vehicles had arrived at the dealership, he took a trip down for an inspection. The vehicles were covered with Cosmoline, a rust preventive substance used to protect cars from salt-water spray during shipment. It would be several days before the cars would be ready for delivery to his place of business.

After the cars were delivered, he still had to wait for Tom to install the radios and roof signs. He had to negotiate with Mr.

Hatchet for a price to paint the logos on the car door panels, as he had no more gaming funds from baseball wagers. Felix was able to negotiate a lower cost per car based on high number of cars.

The Grand Opening of the Virgin Isle Hotel

Virgin Isle Hotel

Prior to the opening of the new Virgin Isle Hotel, Felix had confirmed where his vehicles would park without interrupting the flow of traffic. He had also determined where in the lobby his Silver Streak Service booth would be located. He had already received reservation coupons for expected hotel guests. This was a great advantage as it helped him to plan the driver schedules and to finalize taxi service details for the opening of the hotel in early December, 1950.

Confirmation was needed for vehicles to park at the hotel without interrupting the flow of traffic on the opening day celebration. The evening before opening day, Felix drove up to the hotel. The night watchman knew him and let him drive around the traffic circle in front of the lobby door.

He sat there and silently thanked God for the opportunity to be a part of this premier event. He mentally rehearsed what would take place the next day. He was nervous, but at the same time convinced that he would do a good job.

There was a grand ribbon cutting ceremony for the Virgin Isle Hotel on December 15, 1950. The Governor, Lieutenant Governor, legislators, business, and community leaders and other dignitaries were present, including Jackie Robinson, the first African American signed with the Dodgers major league baseball team, attended this momentous occasion.

A grand tour of the hotel with these dignitaries followed the opening ceremony. Soon a steady flow of guests began to arrive from the airport. Silver Streak Taxi Service drivers wore special tropical colorful shirts and khaki pants for the first week to celebrate opening of the hotel. As the opening ceremony dignitaries and guests departed, three Silver Streak vehicles were positioned in the driveway circle in front of the hotel. Transportation for hotel employees began the same evening.

A hotel doorman, with a whistle, alerted drivers that someone was in need of a taxi. New drivers were assigned to the night shift. They transported the employees to and from work and remained parked at the hotel overnight. Felix kept his pledge to have twenty-four-hour taxi service available at the front door of the hotel. Before the last driver would leave his evening working shift at the hotel, he called the station to ensure coverage.

The Silver Streak Taxi Service information booth was located in the lobby in front of the hotel gift shop. The booth was staffed with a greeter who arranged beach trips, transportation to the airport, and provided information regarding tours and other transportation needs. Initially, all requests for tours were called in to the station and added to schedules of drivers, eventually the greeter assigned customer beach trips, and tours directly to the drivers stationed at the hotel.

In approximately two to three weeks after opening day, the hotel was filled to capacity. Silver Streak Taxi Service had achieved a brisk and steady business. Drivers had to be juggled between location sites to keep up with the heavy volume of business and to cover all taxi service shifts. It was a challenge for Felix to ensure shifts were covered and keep drivers contented.

Tourist business in St. Thomas increased significantly following the opening of the Virgin Isle Hotel. Silver Streak Taxi business flourished with the new hotel contract, local customers, and docking cruise ships. Drivers collected fares from cash paying passengers and submitted coupons collected. Felix paid the drivers sixty-percent of the coupon value. Soon the Silver Streak Taxi drivers became the envy of other taxi drivers. His sister continued to manage the financial aspects for the growing prosperous business.

Felix was able to meet his payroll responsibilities, essential business and loan payment expenses, financially take care of his family, and continue to put aside funds into his savings. With certainty, Felix believed he would be able to recompense his bank loan ahead of schedule.

Purchase of Land on Sugar Estate

The landlord of their apartment informed Felix that she planned to make major renovations to the apartment in approximately two months. He needed to vacate the apartment during that time, but would be welcome to return when renovations were completed. Felix then began to look for a new place.

Once again, he asked his brothers to keep an eye open for word of vacant apartments for his family. A few weeks later, his brother Hidalgo, informed him of a three-bedroom apartment for rent across the street from the school where he worked and close proximity to market square.

Felix made inquiries to the new landlord and arranged to see the apartment the next day. Although the apartment was affable, Felix was concerned about the level of noise emanating from surrounding businesses and lack of yard space for the children to play safely outside. Despite these concerns, Felix arranged to have a month-to-month rental agreement as opposed to an extended lease, because his busy schedule did not allow much time to continue to search for new apartments.

While Felix was in the process of moving his family, he was notified by a friend that the Lockhart family was planning to sell parcels of land in an area known as Sugar Estate. He recalled he had dreams to eventually build a permanent home for his family, but he decided he would inquire about the opportunity to purchase land after his family was settled into their new apartment. After his family was settled into the new apartment, Felix investigated the information he had received regarding the land for sale. He drove approximately a quarter of a mile heading towards the eastern end of the island in search of Sugar Estate.

The area was undeveloped and was known as the "countryside" of St. Thomas. Felix drove around the parcels of land to perceive where he might like to acquire property for a home. He was keen on an area directly across from a dairy where cows were sheltered from the heat under a big licorice tree. He immediately contacted the sellers to put in a bid for two adjacent lots.

Felix did not share his bid to purchase land with his wife. He wanted to wait until his bid for the property was approved. When he received approval to purchase the countryside land parcels, he swelled with pride. He could not wait to surprise his family. He rushed home to tell Huldah the news. She jumped with joy. She wanted to know every detail. Rather than tell the story, he had the family get into the car and drove to the countryside to see where their new home would be built.

The Sugar Estate property began at the bottom of Polyberg Hill. There were no streetlights beyond this point. Although it was dark, on Sixth Street across from the licorice tree, Felix was able to point out their land site with the help of his car lights. He told his wife that he would soon begin to construct blueprints for the new house.

Huldah exclaimed, "Never in my wildest dreams would I have thought I could have anything like this!" Before he drove off, Felix sat in the car not saying a word. He was mentally visualizing what the house would look like on their purchased land.

The next day he told his mother and sister about his plans to build a house on land he had purchased in the countryside of Sugar Estate. He assured his mother that she would have a large room of her own in his new house. His mother and his sister smiled and congratulated him on his newest endeavor. His mother told him there was no need for a room because she was going to die in her own home near the station.

A Major Accident With a Silver Streak Vehicle

Late one evening, Felix received a phone call from one of his drivers. There had been an accident on Raphune Hill involving one of the Silver Streak vehicles. The driver and a passenger were injured. He instructed the driver to contact the wrecker service and to remain at the accident site until he arrived. Felix immediately went to the hospital to check on the conditions of his driver and passenger. He called his wife and informed her as to what had transpired and would keep her informed.

When Felix arrived at the hospital emergency room, he identified himself to the nurse. She verified that the accident victims were there and were being treated but could not release any information on their condition. She advised him to check back in approximately an hour when he would be able to talk with their doctors, and possibly be allowed to visit the patients. He called Huldah to inform her that he was leaving the hospital to go to the accident site. As he drove away from the hospital, he recalled the first Silver Streak vehicle accident of his taxi service business.

One of the taxis had flipped over on the way to Magens Bay. Firemen had to cut the door open to remove the driver. The driver spent a week in the hospital. The car was inoperable and later used as spare parts for other vehicles. He silently prayed that this accident was not as severe. When he arrived at the bottom of the hill, police had stopped traffic from going up or coming down the hill where the accident had accorded.

Parking on the side of the road, Felix identified himself to the policeman and inquired if it was possible for him to walk up to the site of the accident. The policeman allowed Felix to drive up the street behind the wrecker that had just arrived on the scene. When Felix arrived at the site, he saw the vehicle lodged between two large trees.

Fortunately, the two trees had prevented the taxi from going over the steep cliff. The driver and passenger probably would not have survived such a fall over the cliff. When the wrecker pulled the taxi up to the street level, Felix had determined that the vehicle was not a total loss and could be repaired. He paid the wrecker driver and directed him to take the vehicle to Chief's Garage.

Felix headed back to the hospital to check on the injured. While driving back to the hospital, his thoughts returned to the vision of the accident site. He found it hard to believe that the skilled driver could miss the small curve in the road. He needed to find out from the driver what had happened on the road. When he arrived at the hospital, he was informed that the patients had been moved from the emergency room to patient rooms.

Arriving at the room of the driver, a doctor was inside speaking with the family. Felix waited outside the room for an opportunity to speak with the doctor when he exited. He explained to the doctor that the patient was an employee of his company and he would be responsible for any hospital bills. At the front desk, Felix left his contact information before entering the patient's room. He asked the doctor and family members to keep him informed as to the condition of his driver. He later was informed that the passenger was the girlfriend of the driver.

Returning home, Felix was exhausted and went straight to bed. He explained to his wife that he would give an update of the accident in the morning. The smell of breakfast cooking awakened Felix. He sat down to breakfast and gave an account of the accident as reported by the Silver Streak driver. However, he also gave his opinion as to what he thought had occurred with the driver and his passenger. He thought that the driver was teaching his girlfriend how to drive and she lost control of the car.

When he finished breakfast, he told Huldah that he would stop by Chief's Garage to inspect the wreckage of the taxi. Arriving to the station later than usual, Felix repeated details of the accident of the previous evening. Two of the drivers had taken care of his early morning pick-ups and had driven his sister, Elise, to work. Felix remained at the station all morning making changes to the schedule to accommodate the missing driver and car.

Construction of Family Home on Sugar Estate

It was time to begin the task of building his family a home. Felix created a few sketches with preliminary plans and met with the contractor he wanted to build his house. He had selected Mr. Pilgrim, known as "Sappy." They discussed his ideas for the house. Sappy took the sketch and preliminary plans with a promise to return with a detailed blueprint of the new house.

That evening when he arrived home, he told Huldah that Sappy had taken the plans and would return with a professional blueprint. As they discussed what they wanted included in the structure of the house, Felix decided to assemble "his and her" lists. Approximately a week later, Sappy came into the station to discuss the house plans.

Felix took him to his mother's living room where they had more room to spread out and review the blueprint. Sappy presented a materials list and an approximate cost for building materials and labor costs. The overall cost would be less if Felix agreed to have the footings and cistern dug prior to construction of the house. Every home built on the island had to have a cistern to store a supply of rainwater. The houses were constructed with slanted roofs and spouting which would funnel rainwater into the cistern built under the house.

Felix examined the blueprints without saying a word. Sappy asked him what he had thought of the plan and cost. After further review of all paper work, Felix agreed that the plans had encompassed what he had envisioned. He wanted to share the completed blueprint with his wife. He planned to purchase most of the construction materials and fixtures in Puerto Rico and have them shipped to St. Thomas. He planned to pursue a line of credit with a supplier in Puerto Rico, apply for a bank loan, and utilize his savings to fund the project.

Sappy informed him that a down payment of five thousand dollars would be needed to begin the house project. Both men agreed on a financial arrangement to be paid every two weeks. Sappy recommended a man who could dig the cistern and footings.

As soon as Felix arrived home that evening, he showed Huldah the house plans. They both thought the plans were beautiful. Although each room was assessed by dimensions, Huldah was more excited with the size of the kitchen. She hoped and prayed that what they saw on the plans would be a true reality of their dreams for their new home. They were eager for construction to begin immediately.

The next day Felix went to his bank to begin the process for a loan. He contacted prospective construction material suppliers in Puerto Rico. Sappy arranged an appointment for Felix to meet Belford, the man he recommended to dig the cistern and house footings. They met at the station and Felix explained what he needed to be done. Belford agreed to complete the job. He also informed Felix that he would need assistance with the digging. Both men agreed on the cost of the project and start date.

Felix soon had his finances in order and digging for the home project began. A vehicle to tote materials to and from the building site would be necessary. He used one of the local truckers to do the job, but Felix figured it would be cheaper if he had his own vehicle. Tom, a driver and the mechanic, converted an old Woodside Station Wagon into a truck. He cut off the back and removed the seats from the old wagon.

Felix used this vehicle to transport water from the countryside springs for use in mixing the concrete. He placed four fifty-gallon drums in the back. When the drums were filled with water, he placed tree branches over the tops to help prevent the water from splashing. Children who lived in the nearby community and his children looked forward to going on trips to get water to fill the drums and gather tree branches.

Once the cistern and footings were completed, concrete blocks, gravel, and sand were delivered. The plumber had done his preliminary work and framing was about to start. Lumber for framing and the roof were pretreated with a product to prevent termites. Belford treated each piece of lumber and laid them out to dry for a few days before use.

The children were eager to participate in tasks to assist the builders although their mother was not happy with the appearance and the condition of their clothes when they returned home at the end of the day. The wood treatment substance had an unpleasant smell and was very difficult to remove from clothing.

One afternoon, Felix, Huldah, and the children took a ride out to Sugar Estate to see the progress of the house. They were surprised and pleased with the steady and speedy progress of construction. Sappy informed Felix that soon the fixtures and materials he planned to purchase from Puerto Rico would be needed.

Even though Felix was very busy with the taxi service business and monitoring the construction of the house, he enjoyed the challenge. He had to make the trip to Puerto Rico to collect the fixtures and arrange for transport of construction supplies to St. Thomas. While on the trip to Puerto Rico, Felix was able to visit Puerto Rico Tours and personally collect long awaited payments for his taxi business.

When Felix returned from his trip, he had a large number of messages but there were no mishaps. One of the messages was from his card-playing friends. It was an invitation to participate in a high stakes card game on Friday night in the Blue Room at the Virgin Isles Hotel. The entrance fee was two-thousand dollars. He accepted the invitation with a bit of anxiety. He was not in a position to lose that amount of money, but being a gambler, he thought of the possibility of winning a significant amount. He hoped that he would not lose more than his initial entrance fee.

He addressed the other messages, completed the driver schedules for the next day, and drove out to Sugar Estate to check on the progress of the house. Things were looking very good. Felix told the foreman to inform Sappy that the fixtures from Puerto Rico would arrive at the docks for pickup in a few days.

Felix walked around the site checking for any material waste. He had heard and witnessed waste of materials at other building projects and it cost the homeowners more money to complete projects than expected. Felix left the site and headed home. It had been a busy and tiring day. He ate dinner and went to bed early as he would have a busy Friday.

Passing of the Family Matriarch

Felix's mother had not been well. She had experienced chest pains and breathing problems. At the suggestion of doctors in St. Thomas, Felix had taken his mom to see doctors in Puerto Rico. There were not much doctors could do to improve her condition. They prescribed medicine to increase her comfort and improve her ability to breathe.

Upon his return to St. Thomas, Felix had advised his siblings who lived off the island, about the failing health condition of their mother. A few of his brothers had moved away from the island and resided in New York City. Flavel was in the military, and his sister Audrey lived in St. Croix, Virgin Islands. His mother's health deteriorated rapidly after her return from Puerto Rico. Subsequently, Elsa George Vialet passed away on November 12, 1954.

Elise notified her brother of their mother's passing. Felix had previously completed the burial preparations for their father and Elise once again turned to him to assist with burial and ceremony preparations for their mother. She understood that her brother knew exactly what to do.

She notified the authorities of the passing of their mother and called Mr. Maduro to take care of the necessary paperwork to obtain the death certificate. Felix told his sister he would be there in approximately an hour. He relayed the information of his mother's passing to his wife and children. The family members promptly began to cry.

As Felix prepared to leave the house, it suddenly hit him that his mother would no longer be at her home to greet him in the mornings and to say good night in the evenings. Her death was truly going to be difficult to cope with. He prayed that the Lord accepted his mother in his good graces into his Kingdom. He began to prepare for the burial of his mother as he had done for his father. He purchased the blocks of ice from the ice factory and procured the cruder bags.

After he completed these tasks, he departed for the Public Works Department to obtain a burial permit and gravesite. His sister along with family members bathed their mother and he assisted with wrapping her in linen cloth to lie on ice blocks for two days at home before the funeral ceremony and final burial.

It was a blessing to have all of the children present at the funeral ceremony for their mother. Funeral services were held at Elsa's beloved Anglican Church. She was laid to rest across from her husband, Flavel in the Western Cemetery in St. Thomas.

The brothers and sisters were able to come together for dinner several times before they separated again to return to their homes and families. Whenever the children were together, they spoke of their families, reminisced about old times, changes on the island, current jobs, and their future dreams. Felix's only regret was that his mother would not see the completion of his dream home.

The "Blue Room" Poker Game

Approximately three weeks after the passing of his mother, Felix received a second invitation for another poker game to be held at 9 o'clock in the evening in the "Blue Room" of the Virgin Isle Hotel. He had been unable to attend the previous game due to the passing of his mother.

After completing the schedule for drivers for the next day, he headed home. He informed Huldah of his plans for the evening and told her not to worry, as the poker game might be an all-night affair. When Felix arrived at the hotel, he saw a few of his drivers who were on taxi service duty and conveyed that he was meeting friends at the hotel.

He walked pass the front desk to the elevator designated for the "Blue Room." The room was on the top floor of the hotel and all the lights inside were blue. When Felix stepped out of the elevator on the fifth floor, an attendant at the door verified that his name was on the list of invited guests. He was escorted into the room where he paid his "buy in" money and collected his poker chips.

There were two tables set up for six players each. Felix took his seat on the last vacant chair. As people began to lose money and left the game, the remaining players continued to play. At 2:00 o'clock in the morning, there were four players left and Felix was one of them. The group decided that they would stop playing at 3:00 o'clock. The largest pot of money in the early morning was on the poker table. Felix had a great hand and felt he could win it all. His anxiety filled the room. Finally, the game was over. He won the poker pot! He bid farewell and jubilantly looked forward to a return match.

When Felix arrived home, Huldah had awakened. Felix told her that he had won and emptied his pockets onto the bed. He had won eight-thousand dollars. This money would allow him to pay his creditors in Puerto Rico and purchase additional items for the house.

Christmas Festivities and Island Parade

When his mother was alive, Felix was routinely required to complete chores in preparation for the Christmas Holidays. The entire house, or at least the dark green trim around the house, had to be painted. There were many plants in large tin pans around the house. These pans had to have fresh paint for the holidays ahead. Furniture had to be polished and the fabric chair covers had to be replaced.

The week before Christmas, lights were strung around the house. Homes, stores, and streets were decorated. The preparations and impending busy season for Silver Streak Taxi Service helped Felix to cope with the loss of his mother. He knew that he would need assistance to complete some of his chores.

Felix had saved customer holiday reservations from the previous year. He contacted the customers on the list to determine if they would need his services. The previous year his convertible car was commissioned to chauffeur local dignitaries in the annual Christmas Parade.

Parade Car

Felix would have to check with the Chamber of Commerce to inquire whether his special car would be commissioned again by the Christmas Committee for the holidays. He kept the convertible car in a rented garage near the station. He had bought the convertible with winnings from a Baseball World Series bet.

The holiday schedule for his drivers presented special challenges. Drivers wanted time off to spend with their families during the holiday season, but they knew this was the season to make the most money. Felix utilized services of three independent taxi drivers when he had to substitute a driver or when business peaked during the second week of December. During the holiday season, Silver Streak Taxi Service remained open to take calls and reservations until 1:00 o'clock in the morning.

Finally, The Christmas Committee returned his phone call to commission the use of his convertible car for the holiday parade. It was time to get the car clean and shiny. All the chrome was polished and the white wall tires sparkled.

The Grand Marshall of the parade waved to the crowds of people as he sat atop the back of the convertible. Felix heard compliments shouted from the crowds of people as his dazzling car proceeded along the parade route. His slender body frame was swollen with pride.

Night Club Tours Added to Silver Streak Taxi Services

Business was good throughout the end of the year. Felix had to set goals for the coming year. The Silver Streak Taxi Service was in business with approximately forty cars. His taxi service was stationed at five hotels for tours and beach trips. Despite his vast success, there was steady, growing competition in the taxi service business.

Taxi stands were popping up in more areas of the island. With his courteous and calm demeanor, Felix did not cause friction with the rival taxi service drivers. There were times when he had to utilize their private services to support his business when additional assistance was necessary.

The original four-year contract with the Virgin Isle Hotel was soon up for bid again. Felix decided to bid on the contract without any new additions or changes. Another taxi service submitted a lower bid. They were awarded with the hotel contract.

The hotel managers allowed Felix to keep his information booth in the hotel lobby for the guests with prepaid coupons from cruise ships and travel agencies. He was also allowed three designated parking spaces near the tennis courts for drivers waiting to transport these guests with prepaid coupons. Felix had an idea of how to utilize vehicles and drivers formally used with the Virgin Isle Hotel contract.

While guests were in the taxis, they often inquired about nightlife on the island. He gathered information about night entertainment at the various hotels. Each hotel held special activities on different nights. For example, the Virgin Isle Hotel held turtle races on Thursday nights; other hotels had limbo dancing contests or steel band music on other nights. He provided this information to the greeters in the hospitality booths in various hotel lobbies.

Silver Streak Taxi Service would provide a safe way for guests to get to and from the local nightspots. He frequently used station wagon cars to accommodate four couples or eight people comfortably. Drivers picked up customers early in the evening and made two to three stops depending on the type of entertainment sought. The nightclub tour lasted approximately three to four hours.

Soon the night entertainment tours were as popular as day tours and beach trips. The drivers, who were worried about a drop in their income when Silver Streak Taxi Service lost the contract with Virgin Isle Hotel, were thrilled with this new business venture. Felix was astute enough to continually search for new ways to diversify and expand his business.

Completion of Countryside Home and Fifth Move for the Family

Countryside Home on Sugar Estate

Even with all of his involvement with the taxi service business, Felix managed to keep up with the progress of his home under construction. It was time to get the fixtures needed to complete the interior of the house. The house had four bedrooms, two baths, living room, dining room, kitchen, laundry room, and front porch.

Felix went to Puerto Rico to purchase the fixtures and had them shipped to St. Thomas. The builder told him that he expected to be finished in approximately two months. Felix had an additional request for his home. He approached the builder, Sappy, to inquire whether a wall could be built around the perimeter of the property. Sappy thought it was possible as long as the additional construction did not interfere with supply trucks getting into or off site.

Originally, Felix had planned to construct a white cement wall around the house. Later, he found a site on the island that had blue bitch stones. This sturdy stone was native to the islands. Felix thought that the unusual color and durability of the stone would make a beautiful wall in front of his home. Belford, the handyman, dug footings for the wall and Felix had two truckloads of blue bitch stones delivered.

When the house was finally completed, it was time to plan for the move. Furniture had to be purchased. Felix and Huldah went to Soto's Furniture Store to choose furniture and arrange for its delivery. The family packed their belongings and was anxious to move. Prior to the move into the new house, it had to be blessed by the priest. That was the custom in the islands. The family slept in their new home the following weekend. What an exciting time.

Huldah and Felix stood on the porch of their new home and looked west in the direction of the glowing lights from Bluebeard's Castle Hotel. They were both in awe of what had been accomplished. They said a prayer of thanks and went to bed for the first time in their own home.

Transportation Expansion to Island of St. John and Partial Ownership of Virgin Islands Tours

Virgin Islands Tours was one of a few travel agencies in St. Thomas. Felix conducted much business with them with customer with coupons. One day, he was informed by one of the secretaries that it might be possible to own a part of the travel agency. Felix thanked her and attempted to explore the possibility of travel agency ownership. While he was mulling this information over, information about another possible business opportunity arrived.

He had a friend who operated one of the ferryboats traveling between Red Hook dock in St. Thomas and the island of St. John. His friend, Mr. Plaskett, told him that a hotel was being built on Rockefeller property on Caneel Bay on the island of St. John. He also told him that the hotel manager had shared with him an interest in a transportation plan for guests to get to and from the dock in St. Thomas. His friend had recommended Silver Streak Taxi Services.

Felix was interested and told his friend that he would like to meet with the hotel manager to discuss the business further. His thoughts were crammed with ideas and questions about the possible new business ventures. Could he possibly take on more business? How would he finance a partial purchase of a travel agency? He decided to think about it for a few days and then discuss it with wife and his sister.

Within a few days, Mr. Plaskett called to let him know that he had set up a meeting with the manager from Caneel Bay at the Red Hook dock at noon the following day. The meeting would take place on the boat before he made his return trip to St. John. Felix arrived at the dock and waited until all of the guests disembarked.

Mr. Plaskett welcomed him on board and introduced him to the manager. They exchanged pleasantries and then discussed the contract to transport Caneel Bay Hotel guests to and from the airport to Red Hook. In addition, guests needed transportation from Red Hook to downtown and back for day shopping trips. The office of Virgin Islands Tours was the drop off and pick up point.

Felix assured the hotel manager that Silver Streak Taxi Service could meet his needs. They discussed details regarding communication of customer arrivals and departures, the frequency of day shopping trips, flat rates for airport transportation to Red Hook and downtown trips. A tentative agreement was developed. A formal contract would be further developed by hotel management and presented for his approval.

Felix drove back to town with his head buzzing. The prospect of additional business was exciting and challenging. Would he again need to purchase additional vehicles and hire more drivers? How would this new hotel business venture relate to possible partial ownership in Virgin Islands Tours?

He decided to go to the office of Virgin Islands Tours to talk with the owner. Mr. Wilson verified that indeed he was ready to retire. He was willing to split the business into two sections. One section would deal with reservations and ticketing and the other would deal with the coupon business from outside travel agencies.

Felix shared with him that he would be interested in the business section dealing with customer coupons business because he had previous experience in this area. He hoped that he could meet the asking price and if there was another person wanting to purchase the reservation and ticketing business section. Mr. Wilson gave him a figure to consider. He told Felix that there was someone interested in the reservation and ticketing section, and he would set up a meeting with both parties.

It was definitely time to share his ideas and tentative plans with Huldah and his sister Elise. Both women were supportive of his ideas to pursue these new ventures. His sister pointed out that his niece, Juliette, was an employee for Virgin Islands Tours. He could hire her to oversee the customer coupon business. Elise would continue to take care of payroll, business correspondence, banking, and monitor contract development and reviews.

When Felix determined how he would finance the Virgin Islands Tours venture, he contacted Mr. Wilson to inform him that he was interested in his offer for partial ownership of the travel agency. Mr. Wilson called a few days later with a date and time to meet. When Felix arrived, Mr. Wilson introduced him to Mrs. Weber, who was interested in purchasing the reservation and ticketing section of the travel agency business.

Felix and Mrs. Weber knew each other from previous business interactions. The initial purpose of the meeting was for the two parties to discuss how they would conduct both businesses in the same office. Mr. Wilson was comfortable with their ability to have a good working relationship in a single office space. Discussion continued in regards to the division of the office space, telephone access, and furniture arrangement. Felix informed Mr. Wilson that his niece Juliette would be the person to work in the agency office. She had experience and was familiar with customer pre-paid coupons. The meeting went well and Felix was confident that this was the right move to expand and diversify his business further.

After Felix shared the news about his partial ownership in Virgin Islands Tours with the drivers, he arranged to have Juliette meet with them because she would have to interact with them with the customers and distribution of coupons. Soon after he finished negotiating the Virgin Islands Tours contract, he received word that he had been awarded the contract with the Caneel Bay Hotel.

Virgin Islands Tours booked reservations for all guests going to Caneel Bay. This worked out well for Felix because Mrs. Weber was able to inform him of the date and time of guest arrivals and departures. She also informed Juliette concerning guests with prepaid coupons for tours. With this informational arrangement, Felix was better able to prepare assignments and schedules for his drivers.

Many of the Caneel Bay Hotel employees lived in St. Thomas and traveled by boat to St. John daily. With approval from the hotel management, Felix offered transportation to those employees to and from the Red Hook dock. He picked up the employees from the front of the office of Virgin Islands Tours early in the morning and from the Red Hook dock to downtown in the afternoon. He provided this service for approximately three years.

Relocation of Silver Streak Taxi Service Business to Sugar Estate

Felix had decided to move his taxi service business to the location of his home. He slowly began the process when he had the mechanic, Tom, conduct vehicle repairs behind the house. He had planned to erect a building behind his house to accommodate the car repair business. Felix sketched a rough draft of a building that included a two-car garage.

In fact, what he had in mind was a structure that could be converted into a two-bedroom apartment. The front of the structure would be an open space to accommodate two cars and an office. The back of the building would have a bedroom, bathroom, kitchen, and laundry room. He asked his builder Sappy to develop a blueprint to get appropriate building permits. Felix planned to build this garage with the help of Belford, a licensed electrician and a plumber.

The first task was to build a cistern for the structure to have its own water supply. Felix had Belford stopped constructing the blue bitch stonewall around the home property and began to dig for the placement of the new cistern. He was able to get Mrs. Weber's son, Lind, a stonemason, to complete the construction of the wall. It took several months to complete the building, install the gate and the steel accordion doors to the front of the garage. Felix was finally able to move the taxi service business to Sugar Estate.

Garage and Repair Shop

Impact of Canopy Jeeps for Tourists on the Taxi Business

Soon after moving his business to Sugar Estate, Felix started to sense changes in the taxi service business on the island of St. Thomas. The rental car business had been recently introduced to the island. Tropical Motors sold Volkswagens and Jeeps. In addition to car sales, they rented smaller jeeps with canopy tops to tourists who were brave enough to attempt to drive on the left-hand side of the road.

This new form of transportation around the island began to impact taxi service to and from the airport, tours and beach trips. Independent taxi drivers were increasing as people with full time jobs began to taxi in the evenings and weekends to supplement their incomes. The taxi service competition was growing rapidly. Once again, Felix decided that it was time to seek a new way to diversify and broaden his horizons for his business.

By the time that Silver Streak Taxi moved to Sugar Estate, cars in need of repair were on the far side of the house. Tom was no longer dividing his time as a driver and mechanic. He was employed as a full time mechanic for Silver Streak Taxi Service. He was well known on the island for his automotive skills and soon had so many demands for his services that he decided it was time to invest in his own repair shop.

Felix was supportive of Tom's desire to begin his own car repair business. It worked out well for Felix because it meant that he would be able to remove old cars and auto parts from the back of his home. Tom removed cars and auto parts to his new place. Felix removed the remaining old cars and auto parts to an empty lot down the street from the house that he was allowed to access when needed. This lot became known as the "car graveyard."

Once more, Felix had a clever idea to build a small guesthouse on the back area of his property. He envisioned a two-story building with eighteen guest rooms. There was enough space in the yard to install a covered patio where guests could be served a continental breakfast. With his experiences in the taxi and tour business, he knew what guests desired on vacation.

He set out to learn as much as he could about how to operate a guesthouse on the island. He sent letters of inquiry to his contacts in tour agencies in hopes of acquiring their assistance to support his new business venture. This major project involved much planning and funds.

As he explored the feasibility of this endeavor, he realized that securing a water source was a priority. He would need a water supply for construction without depleting his household water supply. There were two spring water wells across the street from his property. He asked his handyman if he thought there might be a water spring on his property. Belford pointed out an area in the back of the property lush with tall grass and other foliage as a possible water source.

Both men were eager to begin a new project after the completion of the garage. With amazing good luck, a water vein was found fourteen feet down! This was very encouraging news. The water supply source gave Felix the impetus to aggressively pursue development of plans for the guesthouse and seek funds to finance his dream. The guesthouse would be known as "Vialet's Villa." His dream became a reality in the year 1960.

Downsizing of the Silver Streak Taxi Service Business

During the construction of the guesthouse, Felix began to downsize the taxi business. At the peak of his taxi service business, he owned fifty-two vehicles and employed approximately fifty-eight employees. It had not been so many years ago that he began with a single car. His business focus was moving in a different direction. He no longer could continue with the present volume of the taxi service business and operate a guesthouse simultaneously.

Travel agencies with which he conducted business were notified of his new plans to discontinue his Silver Streak Taxi Service. Another taxi company was referred to continue taxi service with his contacts at the travel agencies. He sold a few vehicles to individuals and kept enough to continue his contracts with the hotels and provide service to his local customers.

Felix later sold his ownership in Virgin Islands Tours to another local travel agency. In the meantime, he negotiated with the Virgin Islands Office of Tourism to acquire business for the new guesthouse. Felix was enthusiastic to move on to the next chapter in his business career.

Vialet's Villa

Epilogue

"Felix, The Man, and His Car," began with a single idea that developed into a business venture that provided employment for many. My father was a family man who went to extraordinary enterprises to provide for his wife, children and extended family members. He was "a quiet giant" who continually searched for ways to diversify, expand, and improve his businesses.

He progressed from providing services to hotel guests to becoming a guesthouse owner himself. He was a man with progressive thinking who was never afraid to take risks. Not only was he an exquisite role model for me, but for many others on and off the island of St. Thomas, Virgin Islands.

I am so proud that Felix "Skip" Joseph, Sr. was my father. His dreams live on in our hearts and minds.

ABOUT THE AUTHOR

The author, Felix J. Vialet, Jr., called Junior by most of his family was born November 10, 1942, on the island of St. Thomas, United States Virgin Islands to Felix J. Vialet, Sr. and Huldah V. Vialet. They were also the parents of Noreen, Aubrey, and Kenneth Vialet.

Writing his father's story had been a dream of his for quite a few years. He told himself that when he retired that he would seriously seek information on how to get started on writing this story. Felix, Jr., retired in 2009 and became a member of the Lou Walker Senior Center in Lithonia, Georgia. "Writing Your Story" was a program offered at the center. He immediately signed up for the course. Mrs. Estelle Ford Williamson was the class instructor. As an author and publisher, she gave him the impetus needed to take on the challenge of committing this oral history to print.

He wanted to share the story of his father, a humble but ambitious man with ideas who worked hard to realize his dreams. His father started the first Taxi Company Service and Sightseeing Tour Business in St. Thomas, Virgin Islands. Because of these successful business ventures, he not only was able to provide for his family, but also affected the lives of those he employed and the growth of the tourist industry on the island.

Family members and his father's friends were eager and happy to share bits and pieces of his father's life with him. Although Felix Jr. lived through a large part of this story, and knew most of his father's former employees and friends, he relied on all those honest memories to help write this story.

Made in the USA
Las Vegas, NV
13 January 2024